DOGOLOGY 202

Secrets to Living with a High Energy Dog

MATTHEW LAMARAND

ISBN-13: 9781689145534

Dedication

I want to take a moment and dedicate this book as a way to say thank you to all the hard work everyone put in to make this book possible.

I first and foremost want to say thank you to my beautiful, courageous, strong and supportive wife Ashaleena. I want to say thank you for taking a chance on me and providing me the atmosphere to be creative and ability to go after all my crazy ideas and dreams, you will never truly know how much that means to me. I want to say thank you for your help on this book and taking a peek behind the curtain to see how much of a perfectionist I am and allowing me to throw ideas off of you. I know how burdensome and tiresome that is, I want you to know it does not go unnoticed. Without you I know for a fact that this book would still be sitting in my Google docs and the cursor just blinking waiting for my thoughts to be put on paper.

My second dedication is to tell my daughter Natalie thank you. I know daddy sits in the office and does "homework" all day instead of playing with you. I want you to know it will be worth it soon, you already understand that daddy is helping "all the puppies and dogs", but I am trying to build this for you princess. You are the center of my universe and provide the daily motivation I need to get through the tough days mentally and physically. You are strong, confident, independent, creative and a natural born leader that is going to accomplish so much in your life, I feel so blessed that I get a front row ticket to see what is in store for you!

I want to take a moment and say thank you to my mentors, I'm lucky enough to say I have several!

First I want to say thank you to Kathy Tosoain, you are a true role model of how to carry yourself in public with such poise, leadership, class, and patience. You showed me the elegance of how to give captivating public presentations and I will always be in debit to you for that. You have never turned away a broken soul that needs repair or a shoulder to lean on.

I want to thank Landon Porter from The Sales Gorilla. You have shown me that it is ok to be "damaged goods" and still respect myself and what I can accomplish for my clients if I get out of my own way and just do "the thing". To build real relationships with people in my community not to sell shit but to be productive and truly help the community that I live, work and play in. So thank you this book is a reflection of "my weird ass self".

Steven Eugene Kuhn you might not realize it but you have had such a huge impact on my life! I truly felt like a victim of circumstances and that no matter what I do I am destined for failure. As a fellow military veteran you gave me a swift kick in the ass that was so desperately needed. You probably don't even remember that conversation that we had on the phone but you being the gentleman, leader, mentor and class act that you are forced me to pick myself off of the mat and keep swinging against all odds. This book could not have happened without you. Thank you for your foreword you are a true communications professional and seemed like the perfect fit for communicating with our four legged partners.

Steve Shmou of Premier Pet Supply, wow where to begin you took a chance on a kid with an idea and a start up. You gave me advice, an outlet/platform and just the time of day. Thank you so much! I do not know if you know this but my business at the time of our first conversation was not my full time endeavor I was too scared to work for myself, I loved the feeling of the safety net. A week after the conversation and how you just took your leap of faith I walked in and gave my two weeks notice and since then I have not looked back. Seriously, thank you for everything you have done for us!

Amber & Mark Wagenschutz one of the most important clients I have ever had in my entire life! Maggie and Beau were completely different beasts and yet you trusted everything I said. Thank you for giving me confidence that my advice works. You also have been friends and role models about being open about my faith even when I felt the need to turn away from it. You never gave up on me and brought me back from my darkest times. I hope this is a simple way to pay you back but I feel like I owe you more, thank you for everything you have done for us and we strive everyday to be like you guys, in our professional life, as a family, and in our faith.

Table of Contents

Forward

Too often, owners of high-energy dogs live in a war zone of battling bad behavior after bad behavior. Training specific behavioral issues with our dog is like laying the individual bricks of a structure. But the bricks are laid upon a foundation— and if the foundation is weak, the entire structure will be weak. When we cultivate a foundation of a loving, trusting, and respectful relationship with our high-energy dog, this bond becomes the root of our dog's motivation to be our willing partner and follow in our direction.

Many dog training books will tell you how to fix each specific problem. But instead of trying to figure out the hundreds of different solutions to the hundreds of different problems, you can instead learn the Dogology secrets and know how to handle every hurdle that presents itself.

When we become frustrated or angry with our dog, it is not caused by our dog behaving badly, or by our dog being stubborn or stupid. Frustration and anger happen when we don't know what to do— when we've tried everything and are at our wit's end. This is an awful feeling for a dog owner; one laden with guilt and despair.

But we don't have to live in that state of anger and frustration. When we understand the underlying principles of a successful dog relationship, we have a governing plan. We know immediately how to react to every situation, and we do so with knowledge and conviction. And when our dog makes a mistake— as every dog will— we do not become frustrated nor embarrassed by his behavior because we are confident in our technique and ability to best handle the situation. The Dogology secrets empower you with a clear strategy to confidently handle any challenge with your dog.

Kyra Sundance, world-renowned stunt dog performer, NY Times bestselling author

When you think of a book on training and understanding high energy dogs, you don't think of Vincent van Gogh, yet the first line is a quote from this legendary artist. This gives the reader a clear signal that the book is far beyond a typical dog training read.

The parallels between the patience, consistency and methodology of a great artist and a dog owner who seeks to live in harmony with a high energy dog are a fascinating analogy and shows the depth to which the Author Matt believes in and embodies in his art.

A wonderful read for the enthusiast of understanding and embracing true love and understanding for a Man's best friend.

Steven Kuhn
www.Steven-kuhn.com

Introduction

"It is better to be high-spirited even though one makes more mistakes, than to be narrow-minded and all too prudent." ~ Vincent van Gogh.

My first ever book "Dogology 101" was written by me which covered all aspects of living with a dog and being successful at training them in the most efficient way possible. Most of the secrets and sections covered these aspects in a general manner without much specification to the kinds of breeds and their specific needs. To be honest the feedback to my first book was what has motivated me to continue my efforts in the realm of writing as well, along with my practical field of training dogs. Dogology 101 if explained in simple words was all about the "why"; as to why the dogs do what they do and how to be efficient at controlling and manipulating their behavioral needs and aspects in regard to training them.

However, after receiving feedback from my readers and getting enough encouragement to continue with another book I decided to write "**Dogology 202**", but the next thing that was to be decided was what should I write about now? I went through intense analysis of my training sessions with my clients' dogs and then their complaints that they would come to me with, about their dogs and after carefully eliciting the needs of all the people who keep dogs or, are related to training dogs, through my experiences that I gathered by virtue of my work as well as by being social I came upon the fact and the dire need of a guide book containing necessary guidelines and coaching tips for dealing with high energy dogs.

I finally decided to write this book after intense homework, and this book is going to go into the "**how**" after having dealt with "**whys**" in Dogology 101, this book is about living with your high energy dog. I specifically chose this category of dogs because from my experience I had learned about the fact that most of the complaints and problems faced by owners as well as my fellow trainers were somehow related to a breed falling in the category of high energy. Most of the irritated and tired of trying to train and groom their dogs would be owners of high energy breeds whose ultimate dream when they used to come to me was getting their dog to calm own and behave soberly and graciously especially around guests, strangers or kids in the home and would give anything to stop them from destructive behaviors like chewing up the furniture and other things of that nature.

Maybe it will seem unusual to you but unlike many peoples' opinion high energy dogs are my favorite dogs to work with. I can give several reason and justifications to support my choice but top of all would be because they are always willing to please, they are loyal, and they are always the ones to give their unconditional love. They would never be tired of rushing to you when you would call them or command them to a certain action. And not to mention that most of the dog breeds lying in this category are often the fastest learners and one of the most intelligent breeds among dogs, hence giving out maximum to the trainer's efforts.

If you really are one those people who needs distinguishing between the high energy dog and those who are not just ask yourself these few questions, keeping in view your dog's behavior:

Is your dog constantly digging multiple holes in your backyard and is always super excited to get a chance to go out and dig another hole after you filled in your yard?

Does your dog have the habit of constantly jumping on guests in the frenzy of its excitement and scaring your guest to hell?

Does it really get difficult at most of the time to control your dog when you are out with him; does he walk you instead of you walking him or are you always having to run or a chase them whenever you lose hold of the leash?

There can be many more questions and examples that could help determine if you own one these high energy dog breeds. They will require special and more focused training, hence requiring much more consistency and patience out of you along with many other things that you will come to know and learn about in the following sections and along with that, I will be sharing secrets and tips with you that are best at tackling all those problems like a pro and gaining the maximum out of your dog in the minimum amount of the time spent instead of fretting for hours and days and months. yet gaining nothing but meager results.

The first and foremost tip would be to know and accept the dog's behaviors according to its specific breed, and always keep your expectation levels low and spirits high while going for a dog. Most people get dogs based on their looks and not based on their energy levels or need. Dogs are so much more than "furniture" something to look cute and adorable whenever it is appropriate. Dogs are living beings as much as you or I. Once they come to your home they are a part of your family! It is of utmost importance that you research the breed before bringing them into your home. Yes, I realize there are exceptions to the rule, but basic research on the breed or mixed breeds that you are about to get could potentially prepare you for future situations that may arise. Ex. Huskies!! Or Shepherds (Dutch Shepherds look cool but are your mom and dad prepared for one?).

Allyson, the owner of two Rhodesian Ridgebacks, has been a private client, who can practically recite behavioral theory, but she struggled to apply the theories in reality. She understood the basic principle of training her two dogs, rewarding and place and instrumental conditioning but struggled to communicate and apply the dog to return heel.

Section One: Keys to Success

I just became a new parent to a wonderful, beautiful little girl, named Natalie, and much like being a new doggie parent, being a brand new parent to a child is just as hard. I realized that each require the same three things to be successful:

1. It takes an insane amount of patience.

2. It takes a lot of consistency.

3. It takes a ton of structure.

I can well remember getting my first dog when I moved out of my house and was out on my own for the first time. He was a Husky, named Marco, a gorgeous dog with blue eyes, gray/white coat, and full of energy. That first experience taught me many things. I had preconceptions of the dog-human relationship from watching movies or cute animal videos online, where dogs would be well trained and mannered. There was nothing that gave me any clues that I was going to get my carpet spoiled in the middle of a cuddling session or I should be expecting a pile of dog waste at my doorstep or in the middle of my lawn. Little did I know of the struggle that was supposed to be put in to get to the stage where you could allow your dog on you carpet or in the living room without the fear of it getting spoiled or some of your valuable furniture chewed on mercilessly. I had no idea what I was doing. I wanted him to sleep with me, I wanted him to be my best friend, and I thought that if I get him a bowl, a leash, a collar, and go for walks, we'd be good to go.

I can remember our first night with Marco when we brought him home. We tried to put him in the crate at night, and he wailed, screamed, and cried for hours.

That night, everything I had been told, every piece of advice, and every tip that I had gotten from my friends and other sources became a mess in my mind. I could not help worrying about whether it was due to the cold or he wanted to go relieve himself or if it was something else. But my love and passion was new and energetic as well. I woke up probably 10 times worried about him, thinking about him, and wondering what the heck was going on. Every time he cried, I would take him out, thinking that maybe this time all the wailing and crying was really for the need to relieve himself. It was January in Utah in the mountains, and it was freezing cold in the middle of the night, and here I was trying to have this puppy go outside to use the bathroom, and he thought of it as his playtime.

He would just play at my feet, tug on the bottoms of my pants, and play with my shoestrings. I didn't know how to get his attention to get him to go potty. I tried speaking to him and giving all the possible commands remotely related to "go potty" I could think of, but he just kept wanting to play.

In training him, I had the most trouble getting him to relieve himself outside and not in the house. At that time, I heard someone say that the most important trick or thing to get a dog to do to make an owner happy was not to roll when you say "roll" or sit down when you say "sit" or do any trick of any kind, but it would be that he runs and relieves himself outside when you give the command. That was exactly how I was feeling at that time. I would have been the happiest person if that could somehow happen to me.

The most important trick to reach this level is consistency. I learned with time, the biggest mistake people make in regard to training their dog is that they give up too soon. An accident happens during the training, the dog doesn't listen sometimes, and they give up hope. Let me tell you, many times during the training, your carpets or living room will be soiled, and furniture will be chewed on, but if you keep up with the structure and maintain consistency, then eventually, one day, you will have the dog-human relationship you always dreamed of.

Coming back to Marco. After having him for some time, I would put him in the crate when I would go to work. However, with time and after experiencing a few incidents,

I learned that this was also a mistake. Crating him was supposed to restrain and limit his access to the full house in fear of getting my furniture chewed or the house messed up, but little did I know that this was actually causing more issues, such as building a higher drive or layering the high energy that he was experiencing and not getting enough time to relieve that energy. One time, he actually got out of his crate while I was at work and started eating the linoleum in our kitchen, and then he actually started eating into the drywall. When I came home, I found myself in a situation that was very reminiscent of the scene in Marley and Me when John goes to pick up his wife at the airport and when he comes back, he finds that his garage has been trashed. My feelings at the time were exactly the same as those of John. I didn't know how to work with Marco correctly, but I didn't have any other frame of reference, and that was the point when I was near to losing hope. I started calling around, asking for dog trainers in Utah, started looking in Salt Lake City for animal behaviorists, because I knew I was in over my head. Luckily, later, I got accepted into the K9 Academy for the military, and everything started changing and so did my concepts, and I realized what mistakes I was making.

The most simple and basic thing is that you need to work with dogs as you would with a young toddler who doesn't understand English. They learn from the environment; the more structured environment you can provide them with, the stronger the chances that they will learn what you are teaching, and then you need to keep the environment consistent, so the basic training is instilled deep into them for the rest of their lives.

Secret #1: Patience

Experience is a teacher and compared to watching tutorials or getting tips from others, it is something we understand and remember longer. Getting tips from people and then applying them in reality are two completely different things. As I mentioned earlier, achieving your goals requires determination, and to keep determined, one requires above all, patience.

After graduating from the K9 academy, I was assigned my first duty station as a K9 handler in Little Rock AFB, Arkansas. There I met Kato. He was a fully-grown German shepherd. Kato taught me the lesson of patience. He was a military working dog and came from a previous handler who had a different training style than I had. Kato was expecting more from me, but I was a new handler and didn't know anything but the bare basics. Now this is where mistakes are often made by dog owners, especially those who get a grown dog who has been accustomed to a very different set of values and trained by different methods than both the human and dog are expecting.

For example, if you were going to adopt a fully grown child who is in his teen years, then you would not expect him immediately to learn all your values, know what you expect from him in terms of manners, and know all your rules. For his entire lifetime, he has had a set of values learned through different methods.

For a grown dog, when you are expecting him to understand a harsh/loud call as the time to stay or stop, but he has been accustomed to that same harsh/loud call as a signal to attack or start working or maybe when you expect him to start his food on the command of "go," but for his previous instructor, this command was used for signaling that it's time he should relieve himself, this creates confusion and misunderstanding.

The secret is not to expect any dog, and this is true for all creatures, including humans, to completely understand you just in a day or two. I am telling you this, so you don't overwork yourself and stress yourself out because your dog may not be learning as quickly you wish him, even when you have put in hours or days trying to teach him a simple command. It is a process that goes slowly and may take weeks or even months to instill a very basic command and get its expected result from an animal who doesn't understand "English". This concept came to me when I started working with Kato. I expected him to go by my commands, as I thought of him as already trained and didn't expect to put any work into training him for me.

I did go through schooling, and I did learn the science of how dogs learn and what dog training is, but I didn't have the art form down yet. That major hurdle raised the need to practice patience with Kato. Kato wanted to work faster than I was capable, at the time, because he was accustomed to working fast with the previous trainer, but because I did not expect it and hence was not ready for it at all, patience was the only option left for me. This is where I learned that patience was the key to settle your terms with any new dog, especially those that are already grown up.

The thing is that the key of patience goes two ways; first, you need to be patient with the dog, not expecting him to learn everything in a day or two, and second, you need to be patient with yourself, as you cannot also learn all the tricks and theories in just one day. Learning is a process that grows over time and requires patience for all, be it an animal or human. In the beginning, I was too impatient and wanted to learn everything quickly, and due to this haste, I had to face certain failures at times, but eventually, I came to terms with myself and learned to be patient.

Time teaches you many things that many books or other sources cannot. I wanted to do everything faster; I wanted to be better than the seasoned handlers that were there before me. That was just part of my competitiveness, and that might be an issue that you all face as dog owners; you want to have the best trained dog. But you should always remember no good thing happens with only one day's work.

It takes time. It may be several months before you are successful. The first and most important key to training your dog to respond to your wishes and commands successfully is to be patient. Give him/her time to understand you and give yourself time to understand your dog as well. You cannot, in one day, judge that because your dog wails or cries, he needs to go out or that he is hungry.

With Kato, I learned that we should never try to invade the dog's space; rather, we should try to learn his ways, what he understands and how he learns best. For example, does he cares more about a command when given a treat at the end or pay more attention to a certain call or command more than any other? I eventually learned the art of working a dog from Kato, and the biggest factor that contributed to learning that was patience. I got better by leaps and bounds when I tried letting Kato work by his own/already instilled ways and tried not to change him and his ways completely. With time, my relationship with Kato deepened, and eventually, we both developed a very high level of understanding for each other, but I can surely say today that it would not have been possible without patience.

Secret #2: Structure

A long with the importance of patience comes the need for "structure". We can simply explain the term STRUCTURE as the basic boundaries that are set up for an individual. These boundaries are supposed to define what is allowed and what is not allowed for an individual and who belongs where in the whole chain. It outlines what behavior is expected from someone and what response is expected from others.

Structure is, by far, the most important element in the military. It defines our rank, it defines our customs and courtesy, and it defines how we conduct ourselves with each other daily in the armed forces.

Because of that, what my time in the military taught me defines what I think of as necessary. It's a must to have a structure in our household for everyone, and that includes our dog. This doesn't negate Cesar Milan and the Alpha Dog mentality, but you do have to have a clear structure of what is allowed in your home and what is not; for example, surely it would not be allowed for your dog to get into the kitchen and go around licking the utensils. As a personal example, my dog, Vodnik, is not allowed to bare his teeth or growl at my daughter. That doesn't mean my daughter is an alpha; it is the basic hierarchy of command that must to be put in place. I don't use alpha as an everyday language, but there are certain acceptable behaviors for him to conduct himself, and then there are certain behaviors that are totally unacceptable. Growling and baring his teeth will never be acceptable to family members and any guests that we may have. On the other hand, as a response to that behavior that is expected out of Vodnik, our daughter is not allowed to grab Vodnik's tail or jump on him, or do any kind of action that may provoke any of these behaviors from him. It's just a controlled, structured environment that we must provide to raise our dogs and our children. It is like the basics of disciplining. And discipline is what will bring relief and structure in your life.

Then comes the connection of structure and patience; you certainly cannot inculcate structure to your dog in a day or two and let him know what all is expected and what all is not expected out of him in plain English. You need to be consistent in your teaching and be patient. I have already mentioned that it's a process, and it will take time.

You may fantasize about being the person in an advertisement or a movie with his well-mannered dog, who knows how to behave with whom and never crosses the limits set out for him, but if you hope to adopt a dog and expect such behavior from him that same very day, you are going to be sadly disappointed. Without spending numerous strenuous days working with your dog and without actually knowing how to instill those behaviors in him and teach him the basic structure of your house, which is an environment completely new to him, then you cannot expect much from him. Rather, you should be expecting a scene such as this:

Coming home after a long day of work, you find your furniture destroyed or your living room soiled. When family, friends, or strangers come over, your dog has no inhibition control and jumps all over them, and he has no regard for your commands when he is excited or has aggressive tendencies because it's possessive of its home or toys.

This is because you always see a well-mannered dog behaving perfectly with his owner and all those around him in the movies, but the problem is that you are unable to look at the hard and strenuous weeks or months of training that his owner or trainer had to put in to reach this stage.

I wanted Vodnik to be my demo dog for my business; I wanted him to be my demo dog for the good behavior as a result of my training, but he always gave the demo of otherwise behavior. I wanted him to represent Dogology University gracefully, but every time I would let him outside in the beginning, it was very difficult for me to control his rush of excitement or his jumping up at me or anyone with a treat in his or her hand. It took a lot of patience and time to teach him the basic structure of everything at my business place and my home etc.

In looking back to the place where Vodnik was bred, he had eight brothers and sisters, and he learned his initial habit of going potty from there. I'm pretty sure they used potty pads when he was growing up before he came to me. This is what I could make out from his behavior. Whenever he would come back inside after I had let him out for some time with the intention that he may relieve himself, contrary to my expectations, he would come back in, find a corner, and use the bathroom there. That habit of his instilled in me the levels of patience I did not know I had. Getting your living room soiled daily can be pretty infuriating for anybody, and it took all the patience I had to not wipe his nose in it, or to scold him, or to reprimand him. But this patience and the structure I wanted to instill is exactly what also led me to success.

I remained determined and kept doing the same exact thing. I would pick him up every time he would start doing potty in the corner and would run outside and place him there, and if he finished there, I would reward him. This way, I gradually instilled in him the sense that he is supposed to relieve himself outside and not in the house and that the home is not the place for him to potty, but it is place where he is supposed to live. It didn't happen after once or twice or even three times, and it was a process that I had trust would eventually pay off one day. It took me a month or more to get near to success in instilling in him the habit of doing potty outside the house.

My experience taught me well the importance of the basic structure necessary to be reinforced with a dog and then the patience required for it.

Secret #3: Consistency

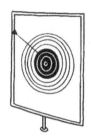

What is onsistency in dog training, and how important is it? Well, being consistent means we have the same expectations and punishments regardless of the situation. This means we have to overlook and curb our instantaneous behaviors and reactions to certain situations and stay strong, determined, and tuned in to what we are trying to teach our dog and how we are trying to teach him that. Behaving in a certain way to your dog or some of his actions at a certain time when you are in a good mood and then behaving totally opposite when you are just not in the mood is a definition for being inconsistent.

You know what inconsistency is? Inconsistency is when you tell your dog to go back to his mat, but he is begging you through his eyes that he wants a place beside you on your sofa or bed. Sure it looks cute, a nice, clean dog sitting right beside you, but you just can't allow your dog to do that at certain times and then not let him do it on other occasions.

A dog must know what places he can visit in the house and what places are just not allowed for him, for example the kitchen, and he can only learn this if you remain consistent in your training. The key is to follow the same at all times, regardless of the situation and your desires.

This brings me to the topic of dog begging. If your dog is constantly begging, it's probably because you set the expectation that he's allowed to have human food when you're eating. If you can honestly say that you've never given your dog any table scraps, but he is begging while you are eating, someone in your household has done it previously. That is another example of inconsistency. To get upset about it is inconsistent yet again.

With these inconsistencies, we're setting up your dog for confusion. We're going to reprimand him for one thing but praise him for the same exact thing at another time? Or, praise him for something but then immediately reprimand him when he tries to get our attention by doing the same thing again? That's not fair. It's going to lead to confusion; it's going to lead to frustration, and above all, it's going to lead to resentment from your dog.

Consistency can be easily understood in the context of some examples of parenting. If I tell my daughter that she has to take a nap at a certain time, but my wife says, "No, you don't have to go to sleep at 1:00 and you can stay up and color, or you can play quietly," it's inconsistent with what I'm saying and vice versa. If my wife says, "You can't watch TV while we're eating dinner," but then when my wife's not around, I allow Natalie to watch TV while she's eating, she doesn't know what to expect, and it leads to fear, and we would end up confusing our daughter on what's right and what's not, which leads to resentment between my wife and me and then between my daughter and me.

Bringing it back to dog training, when I had Kato, Kato had a very poor response to the patrol work exercise for building searching. What we expect our dog to do for the building search is, whenever it finds the suspect and it's behind a door, the dog needs to scratch an alert on the door. Kato was consistently being passive at the door when we needed him to be aggressive. I had to be patient, structure out the exercise, and be consistent with my patterns. I tried my best not to be inconsistent by any means, in the giving the command, giving the treat, and all other factors involved in that exercise. I waited for a response from him and then rewarded him with a treat. This, in retrospect, were all three principles to the keys to success. When all three were in play, we were able to get Kato to aggress and show that same response towards the door each and every time, which was great for me, because it gave me the confidence in working with Kato out on the road for real world situations.

For dog owners, this can eventually be applied the same way for situations such as leaving them out of a crate all night, or leaving them outside of the crate when you leave for most of the day, or just being confident in his behavior with strangers or other dogs when being introduced to them or when you're not there.

Consistency means you will have to work hard - not for just a week or a month - it may take you much longer than you are expecting. Because if you live in a family, all the members of the family have to be on the same page about how to treat your dog. You can't just tell your dog one thing, while other family members are telling him something else.

Different commands to a dog from different members of the family will always lead to confusion about what he must do and what he is prohibited from doing. All dogs are not the same. Some may learn what you are teaching them in a span of a month or two, and for some, it may take six months or more, but once again, patience and consistency are necessary during this process. You'll have to be consistent about what you want to teach your dog and the way you teach him. The method, the prize, the punishment must remain same throughout the whole process.

Section Two: Self-Awareness

What do we mean by being self-aware, and what is self-awareness in regard to dog training? Being self-aware refers to anddemands the point that one must know the conditions and the circumstances around him at any period or moment that may affect or count to what he is trying to achieve in that particular moment or instant. Being self-aware demands that one should not ignore or bypass, at even a single moment, anything that may conflict with his or her desired goal or miss anything that may hold any importance in that regard.

How does being self-aware affect dog training and what role does it play in this regard? Self-awareness is an important aspect while training a dog, as it plays a pivotal role in avoiding confusion in the dog, building up behavioral problems, or evading reluctance in the training session etc.

We all know that one person or an animal who is not self-aware. For me, that person is named "Kat". Kat is a relative, a co-worker, a peer, a strange at the bar who would get in my personal space and never learn that I don't like it. No matter how I would react or give social cues to tell them. They do the same rude things over and over again and find learning difficult. They never know their strengths or weaknesses and don't understand why people are hesitant about working with them. In a nutshell, they are not very aware about themselves and the social demands that are often required.

But dogs are not like cats. They are more intelligent and are fast learners. We can say they possess higher levels of self-awareness. They are always ready to train and seek true happiness in learning ways and means to please their owners or trainers. They understand their environment in a much better way, learn from their mistakes, and if properly told so, they tend not to repeat it.

So when it comes to dog training, I am of the opinion that it is not always the dog's fault. When we are at the initial stages of dog training, we can make certain mistakes that may lead to wrong understanding or concept development in dogs regarding how we introduce the commands, the rewards, the leash, the pressure, or anything of that nature. I am not saying that humans have lesser levels of self-awareness than dogs, but I can say for sure that humans do get careless and, at times, clumsy in their habits and hence make such mistakes without realizing, making them fall in the category of not being self-aware.

It can be simply explained with the example that, when we are trying to teach a "down", but we are giving an upward pressure of the collar and leash, the dog is hesitant about going down. It doesn't want to feel that pressure, so it refuses to get into the four paws down position. This is just one example, and this concept can be further elaborated by many other examples that one may face while trying to train his dog.

When I first picked up Kato, Kato had a tendency to break a stay and crawl towards me. Kato would be in a down position; I would tell him to stay, and I would turn my back towards him and start walking away, and when I turned back towards him, he would have broken his stay and already moved. What I didn't realize was that I was actually stepping off on the wrong foot, which was the same foot that is given to initiate the heel position.

Instead of stepping off and walking with my right foot, I would give him a stay command and step off like we were marching with my left foot. He was conditioned through years of training to march when the trainer would start walking on his left side. I had very little self-awareness at this time, and my consistency to his previous training was nowhere near where it needed to be, as I was giving him the command to march without even realizing it.

I had so little self-awareness that there'd be times Kato would be telling me what he was expecting, or that he was in odor, or that I was giving him the wrong command and so on. I didn't know about this at first; it's something that takes time and patience to understand.

Even though dogs have very little self-awareness as defined by the recent researches conducted, sometimes humans are even less self-aware of the way they are training their dog and whether it is right or not.

Most mistakes regarding self-awareness are done during leash manipulations. A trainer must be aware of his actions and expectations. You just can't pull the leash upwards while you are commanding your dog to sit down; the dog will always try to avoid the pressure and may get confused about the whole process.

Lack of self-awareness may lead to problems, such as creating confusion for the dog, eventually frustrating him. But one can't overcome his mistakes or weaknesses in just a day. As I said earlier, it's a process and requires time and asks for patience and consistency. The best way to remain self-aware is not to proceed with the training without a proper plan. Always structure out the training plan, remain consistent to it, and be patient for the results. Do not mix two exercises with each other, even unconsciously; like the mistake I used to do with Kato while training him. You should always be very conscious of your actions along with your verbal commands or leash manipulations etc. Lack of consciousness may have adverse effects for the training, resulting in resentment and frustration of the dog.

Secret #4: Leash Manipulation

In the earlier part of this section, I explained how important being self-aware is while training your dog and common mistakes that we make in this regard. Going further in-depth of self-awareness in regard to training a dog, leash manipulation is probably the most important part. If leash manipulations are properly learned before practically applying them in your dog-training session and are executed efficiently, we can very easily and effectively teach our dogs to follow the pressure of the leash and collar, making the overall job much easier for them and us. Leash manipulations make dog training easier, not in regard to just one particular act, but many. These include heeling, sitting, returning to heel, coming, and things of that nature.

Now we will discuss how it is supposed to be done and some important points that are to be taken care of while applying them practically with your dog in training sessions. Let's start with an example; if we're trying to get our dog to heel, but at the same time we are pulling the leash backwards (in the opposite direction the dog is supposed to go if he is to follow your command), the dog is going to follow the pressure towards the pull of the leash and may get confused between the command we are giving and the pressure he feels in regard to the leash or collar.

Another example to explain this can be when we are trying to get our dog to down, but we're putting pressure upwards through his leash; the dog is instinctively going to go into a sit position following the pressure, and so on. If we try to put him into a sit, but we're pushing pressure downwards, the dog is going to want to avoid that pressure or may presume that we mean for him to go into a down position. At the same time, if we are careful in regard to leash pulls and remain self-aware of our movements in regard to our dog's leash, it may help us let him understand the command more easily and sooner.

If we have refrained from doing all these exercises regarding leash manipulations and have not done any type of pressure on/pressure off with leashes, and we have become dependent on retractable leashes, this is where we start losing control and command over our dog. This is when we get the maniac pulling of dogs, eventually leading to dogs that do not care about the pressure because they have come to realize that they can go away in the direction and place of their choice if they pull hard enough. This means that whenever we put them on gentle leads or gentle harnesses or tools that are band aids, they do not really help solve the behavioral issue of pulling; rather, they may worsen it. Dogs, like all other animals, need to learn that they are dependent on their owner's commands and are not independent in their actions. This is not to assert some kind of orthodox thinking, but this is very important for the safety of other people as well themselves (the dogs). The moment a dog realizes that he can do whatever he feels like, this is the end of the training for him. This behavior of pulling hysterically compounds until the owner or the caretaker of the dog no longer feels inclined to take the dog out or hesitates to avoid the odd situations it may lead to and then even worse happens; the dog is left in the house to build up even more energy and becomes a higher risk of becoming a higher energy dog with destructive behaviors. I understand that leash manipulation can be hard and monotonous, but it is something that is needed. I've been told that I have made dog training look extremely easy. That's just based on people seeing me interact with dogs and manipulate the leash to get the dog to do what I need it to do. It wasn't always like this, though.

I can never forget the first time I used a 360 leash, which is a long line for tracking and scouting decoys or bad guys. I was in San Antonio at the academy and using it, and I was using the Dutch Shepherd, named Flint. He was a heavy dog of about 80 pounds, and I lost track of how much leash I actually had. What happened is that it got wrapped up around my leg, and when Flint actually caught odor of the decoy, he pulled as hard as he could, resulting in ripping up my legs. My back was flush with the ground, and I fell smack on my back and had the wind knocked out of me for a moment. After that, I learned how important keeping up with your leash is, let alone leash manipulation, to get the dog to obey commands easily.

Leash manipulation is probably one of the most important things that a dog trainer must know. Its proper knowledge provides the owner with a greater ease to train his dog, and if not properly done, it may result in accidents at certain times, resulting in injury of the owner as well as others, like the one that happened with me with Flint.

When learning this art, leash manipulation is probably the hardest part of the dog training to learn. But if one remains consistent, self-aware, and patient, it can eventually be done efficiently.

A trainer must be aware of his leash at all times and should keep his commands and leash manipulations in synchronization and focused on even the most minor details.

As summarized, leash manipulation can make the dog training easier and quicker if used properly and vice versa if not used properly. It is probably one of the most important parts of dog training that a trainer must learn and work on with patience and consistency, while remaining self-aware.

Secret #5: Body Positioning

The next important thing that comes into play regarding self-awareness while training your dog is body positioning. As I have said, the levels of self-awareness in dogs are quite higher than other animals. This implies that they pay attention to their environment much better than their competitors, i.e., other pets and often their owners. They pay attention to the minutest of things that are occurring around them. They have elevated levels of attention, especially during training sessions, as it is the time for them to win their owner and get some yummy treats and toys.

If body positioning is ignored or not given enough importance during training sessions, then this may lead to ineffective communication of commands from trainer to the owner, and this can resultantly effect the efficiency of the overall training process, however, if catered to carefully and executed properly, this can greatly help in training sessions.

I have seen plenty of clients who move themselves into a certain position after a command is given and then reward the dog. Let me give an example to make it easier to comprehend: I have seen some of my clients giving the command heel, and instead of waiting for the dog to come to them and giving the dog some time to position its front shoulder blades to the owner's legs, the owners position themselves to the dog's shoulders, and then they reward the dog. In this way, instead of teaching the dog what to do, the owner gets to do all the work, and the dog, without even doing anything, gets rewarded without even knowing what they did to get it because actually they have not done anything at all. I don't think that makes sense; what are we teaching our dogs at that point?

We always have to be clear about our commands and what they are supposed to teach our dog or what is expected out of a dog when it is given. Similarly, by making this mistake, changing our position to align with the dog instead of letting him do it, we are just making him come to us. So we need to ask this question from ourselves: what do we want from them when a command to heel is given? It kind of gets funny at this point that, instead of letting our dog heel, we are doing so in his place. At this point, I will assume that you know what the command is, but we need the dog to be obedient.

I have also seen an Airedale, who the owner would tell to come, but the Airedale always came halfway and then stopped there instead of reaching us. He never actually fully came up to me or the owner, and initially, I had to take a step back and ask the owner, "Could you give him the come command one more time?" At this place, I noticed that the owner would break the position where he was staying, and instead of waiting for the dog to come forward to him, he would move to the dog to reward him. This was the mistake the owner had been making, not being self-aware of his action and its impact on training his dog. The dog had actually become obedient to come, but he had been conditioned to stop halfway at the command because that was where he was rewarded by his owner, instead of reeling the dog in on a leash, using leash manipulation, and then waiting for the dog to get in position.

In my career, I have also seen treats being held in awkward positions by owners for the dog to unlock the reward. This practice is very prevalent with the smaller, high energy dogs, such as Jack Russell's or any of the puppies. If the reward is held too high, the dog then jumps up to get to it. Then, the dog might steal one and gets rewarded. We do not know that, though unintentionally, we have reinforced the jumping behavior to our dog by giving him rewards for this action or behavior, which then can compound over time and become a larger issue.

Something that has also happened is in the heel position; instead of trusting the dog will be flush with the owner's legs, the owner will look backwards and down to see if it's there, and then when they look down, they are actually seeing that the dog is in position, and they reward him. But in reality, what happens is that the dog has been conditioned to move on this very body action of his owner and wait for it to happen. He is actually further behind and is waiting there for the owner to look backwards and then he would move toward his owner to heel, as he has been conditioned to do over time

The whole idea of body positioning and its role and importance regarding training your dog can be summarized as that we, as owners and/or trainers, always have to be careful and self-aware of what we are trying to teach our dog and how are we moving and what body position we are always in while giving the command. As I have mentioned, they notice and pay attention to the tiniest details of their environment, especially when their owner is interacting with them. Hence, we have to be very careful during training sessions regarding our body positioning, as our carelessness may result in conditioning our dog for a certain command to that very posture, without even realizing it. This may lead to frustration in the trainer or owner as to why their dog is behaving in a way that they have not taught him (which actually they have done themselves unknowingly), as well as confusion for the dog, which may create resentment in the dog to training sessions over time.

Secret #6: Reward Timing

What is most important to be kept in mind while rewarding a dog? To me, the most important thing that is to be kept in mind while rewarding a dog is that he understands and knows very clearly without any doubt or confusion what he has been rewarded for. He should be made very much aware of the action he has done that resulted in getting rewarded.

This is vital while training your dog because this is the only way the dog is going to stick to doing a certain action that is required when a certain command is given to him. Just think, for example, if you are giving a command word to your dog for heel and he has just come to you from a distance and has not settled into heel position yet properly and you give him a reward too early. This may lead to making the dog think or assume that he just has to come over to you as a response, which is required out of your command and to earn him a reward. And worse is, if this habit or mistake is not realized and corrected timely, your dog may get conditioned to doing a half action or incompletely responding to a command. The simple thing to understand here is that we are supposed to let our dog know by giving him a reward that he has successfully followed the command and is always supposed to do so whenever such a command is given, but if we reward him too early or too late while he is in the middle of doing something different, he may link that action to your command.

Second, it is important to get your dog's focus before rewarding him. For the owner or trainer, it is very important and holds great significance to keep in mind with training the "look at me" command or training him to make eye contact. The eye contact and "look at me" command is really just to get the dog to focus in on you. It is very important to get his attention before proceeding with teaching certain difficult commands or introducing commands that are highly distracting or when we have to work with our dogs in a highly stimulating environment and are going to teach him certain commands in that kind of environment. Getting your dog's focus and attention before teaching him something new is important because we don't want to give a new command to our dog or introduce something new to him when he is not paying us full attention and is distracted by certain other things around him. It is very important to let the dog know the importance of the word of command and instill the fact into his mind that ignoring a command is not an option. Seeking your dog's focus and complete attention may greatly help us get our dog to do as is expected out of our command. It is just like a child needs to pay attention to his teacher and focus on the lecture to fully learn whatever the teacher is trying to teach him.

It is also crucial, whenever we are teaching our dogs any new commands, we do not reward him too early or too late. Rewarding your dog too early, before he has even completed the task or what he was supposed to do on the word of command, may lead our dog to link the command with the wrong action, sometimes stopping in the midway or sometimes not getting it at all. Because of this, we would have to give the command more than once, and repeating your commands over and over just leads to a rabbit hole of issues down the line, the most simplest of which is that the word used for command gets too light on his ears to make him or her follow it. Second, if we reward him too late, even after he has completely followed the command, he could actually break the position and repeat that cycle of not being in the position that we want it to be in, and we reward him when his focus is distributed to certain other things, so he could again attach or mentally link the command to something else. Then we have to repeat ourselves and again, going down a rabbit hole of behavioral issues down the line. The best course of action would be to get your dog's attention and teach them the command effectively the very first time.

This is something that I had learned from my experience during my military service, especially with the German shepherd Kato that I have mentioned in an earlier section of this book. Reward timings and their usage was very prevalent with Kato and me when we were doing detection for explosives. If I rewarded him too early, and I saw a change of behavior, this would lead to a fringe response, meaning he is not directly in odor, but the second he would smell something, he would sit, indicating to me that we are in for something. And when we'd call the EOD, it would not actually be there, and it would cause a host of issues. Similarly, if I rewarded him too late, on the other hand, and had not rewarded him once he had successfully followed the command, he would then take it as this command was not supposed to be for what he had done, so he would second guess himself and see if he could get into odor even further or give up all together. In a nutshell, to keep our dogs engaged and train them efficiently to our commands, we have to keep the reward timing pretty consistent and be very clear about our commands and what is supposed to be done by the dog on that specific command. We should keep in mind this simple rule in regard to reward timing: **"Not too early, not too late."**

Secret #7: Controlling the Environment

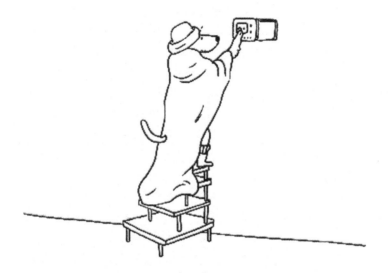

The importance of controlling the environment and how to do it is my all-time favorite topic for training a high energy dog. The concept of controlling the environment can be understood by considering a daily parenting example. Just think of yourself as a parent of a child, who roams around their home all the time. In such a scenario, we would never just let our children crawl all about here and there and get into stuff that could possibly hurt them or cause ruckus or damage.

Controlling the environment is all about controlling our environment and surroundings in such a way that our kids or any dependents should not reach items that may cause them harm or they may damage. We plan and arrange their environment, and that includes restricting their access to different items and places in such a way to avoid any untoward incidents. For example, we would lock up the kitchen cabinets where we keep the cleaning supplies to keep our kids from reaching them; we keep up baby gates to keep them off the stairs to keep them from any harm from falling or slipping off the stairs, and when they were younger, we actually used to keep them in a very controlled environment, such as a playpen.

Now, applying all the same explanations and examples for dogs, we can do the exact same thing with our dogs in areas that we don't really want them in by controlling their access to those places, especially if they are a puppy or they are one of the high energy breeds and have the tendency and ability to jump up on our counters where we keep our food. Baby gates can be considered an easy solution to control the access of your dog to such areas. If possible, you can put up a baby gate to prevent your dog from going into the kitchen and reaching places meant for food and places you do not want your dog to get to, or you can put up a baby gate to prevent them from going into the bathroom and drinking out of the toilet.

Controlling the environment is also vitally important in the night time and times of day when we can't constantly keep an eye on them or the places where it is difficult to keep them under supervision around the clock.

One of the most difficult things to train a dog to do and one of the most important ones as well is potty training. As I have mentioned earlier, it is the foremost thing that a dog owner wants his dog to learn and rid himself of coming in to the sight of his living area soiled and so on. One of the most efficient ways to get on with potty training and eventually achieve your desired goal regarding this very aspect is controlling the environment of your dog.

It is a well-known fact that a dog would never soil or litter in the place where he lives. Reducing that area, for example keeping your dog in a cage in the initial stages of potty training, can help achieve this goal.

Young puppies have very weak bladder control, and it is difficult for them to hold for longer times, so if they get a large enough area, they would find a nook or a corner, even if caged in a bigger space, and would do their business. This especially happens at night time often when the owners does not want to get up from bed and take them out to potty. What happens is that, if we keep them in a bigger crate at night, they will then not potty where they sleep, but if they have enough space to themselves to roam or move around, then as I said earlier, they will find a corner in the crate and use the bathroom there. If such an incident happens and counter measures are not taken in a timely manner, then it is going to be very, very difficult to prevent them from continually going there as they age.

Along with this comes another factor of controlling the environment; that is the smell. It is agreed that dogs do have a strong sense of smell. Consider a scenario: if we do not effectively clean their waste immediately to the extent that the odor of the waste is removed completely from a spot or any particular place where they have littered, but we did not want them to go potty there, then due to that smell or odor of their waste, they would designate that area permanently for doing their business.

Controlling the environment also helps us in training our dog, especially at the very initial stages, when it is very hard to get your dog's full attention and even the slightest distraction can take his attention away from your commands and the work you are putting in him goes to waste. When we control the environment, we can control the level of any distractions present in that environment as well. We are not going to add too many distractions in the early stages of basic training sessions, and then we can gradually increase them over time as your dog gets better at keeping his attention to you during training.

We are not going to add too much stimulation, keeping it to the levels that we are going to be able to control easily without losing the focus of the dog on our commands and instructions and rewarding them on the behaviors that we are teaching.

If we introduce too many variables in an environment or try to teach a dog several things together, we won't know what the dog is responding to and what it is actually understanding, so it is recommended to shape and plan the environment according to what we are trying to teach our dog and then start with the training session, keeping a very tight check on any disturbances or attention deviators etc.

Section Three: Power of Our Words

What is the first thing that comes to your mind when you think about dogs? Even those, with the least knowledge of dogs know and accept the fact that they are the utmost faithful creatures. To me, the first thing that comes to my mind is a creature wagging his or her tail with insane excitement, doing stupid things to earn some praise from his companion or make him happy. Striving for praise from others is not something that is limited to dogs, but we, as humans, also love to get sincere appreciation for our deeds and work, and at times, we are relentless to earn it, just like our dogs. Our dogs love to see us pleased; pleasing his or her owner is the utmost important thing that exists in a dog's mind, and for this, he can go to limits that we cannot even conceive. They are the kind of creatures that give unconditional love and faithfulness, so if we can show excitement or show appreciation for their good behaviors and reciprocate their love and affection, then surely it would go a long way. The more love you show for your dog and the more affection that flows from your words, the more your dog gets determined to stick to his good behaviors, and not only that, but you will see that, over time, your dog will always strive to make you more and more happy, just to be in your company and presence.

After stressing about the show of love and affection and their importance for your dog, we come to the point where we learn how we can translate our love and affection for our dog in such a language or symbols that is easier for our dog to comprehend as love and words of praise. Surely, the dog will not understand our English or whichever basic language we speak, and somehow, we will have to learn ways and means by which we could translate our love or praise for our dog. Take it like an example of an interface or a bridge between two incompatible things, with us standing on one edge of the bridge and our dog standing on the other edge, and the bridge is what makes communication and comprehension for each other possible and easier. If we say it in dog training terminology, we will need to do certain actions; we will need to speak or talk in certain patterns - making sure we are sure of the pitch of our voice, the excitement in our actions, and going to the extent that we should be careful about how we act or behave even with others in our dog's presence. They are even aware about the love you have for them by watching your eyes.

Consider this example; have you ever seen a dog respond to someone who gives them baby voices or communicates just with baby voices? You have surely noticed that they get pretty excited by these high- pitched and excited voices, and they comprehend or translate them as their owner's happiness or excitement. And in response, you have (in most of the cases, because at times the level of attention that each dog is giving to his owner varies greatly from other dogs) noticed that they usually wag their tail full of excitement and actually come back for more pets, seeking more attention and affection from their companion.

This is the secret tactic that I employ with new dogs. Whenever I meet a new dog, that is how I play with them at first. I use baby voices, which helps me translate the message of love I have for them and makes them relax, fading away their worries and the tense environment that is created when a new person meets a particular dog. I want them to understand that I am not a threat. I might be bigger than them or I might have a deeper voice than what they are accustomed to, but I can give them the same excitement that their parents give back at their home.

This reminds me of when I picked up Kato for the first time (the German shepherd that I had to work with during my military training as I have mentioned in earlier sections). As I was starting to get in a routine with him, I don't exactly remember how, but somehow, I came up with a puppy song. If you have been one of my clients, you would have surely heard me sing this song. Eventually, this is what became a sign for him that I was praising him or expressing my affection for him, and he would always respond to me full of excitement and joy. I have certain videos of me opening the gate while singing this song and Kato, upon hearing me, running down the aisle to go outside. I would continue to sing the song, and he would become more and more excited, showing all his internal joy and happiness with super excited dances; he would spin in circles, and most of the time, would greet me unconditionally.

This is just one of several examples that I have experienced in my career while interacting with dogs, may it be during training sessions or living in my routine with one of my own. This is how important the power of words is; you can just see that the excitement and the enthusiasm in my words or in my speech, or just speaking to your dog in a voice in a certain pitch that shows excitement or love, are actually affecting his behavior for the good of it, and this goes the other way around as well. Too dark or harsh voices may make him repressive in his feelings, leading to depression, aggressiveness, and other dangerous behaviors. It is an amazing thing, and it is something to keep in mind. The power of our words and our voice inflection can really dictate how our training sessions can go.

Secret #8: Marking Words

The next important thing that comes while training a dog is marking words. What is a marking word and why are they used? What importance do they hold in training a dog? The answers to these questions are as important as anything else while training a dog. So, starting with the first question, a marking word in our instance is to let the dog know what we are actually expecting from him during any training session, whenever a certain command is given to him and then reinforcing that command through a certain word to condition your dog about whether your dog has done as per your desires or has gone against it.

Starting with a simple example, consider a situation during one of your training sessions with the dog when you give a chain of commands to him or her, such as sit, down, come, heel, and the dog is repeatedly doing all the commands that we have asked in that exact same order, and then we rejoice at the way he has been obedient and pay great attention to our commands, praising him and telling him in a way that he has done a great job. We are going to say, "Good, Good boy, Good job." So if you have focused on the last sentence, you would have noticed that "Good" is our **marking word**. It is the word that marks the good behavior notification shown by the dog and communicates our happiness in this regard to our dog. This marking word acts as a bridge to our next command. The sequence would go: "Sit, Good, Down, Good, Come, Good, Heel, Good..." and so on.

As you can see, I am not using, "Yes" at all during this sequence. Yes is used as a breaker when we are actually going to break the dog from obedience and reward them for the behavior being concluded. There is another breaker I use; that is "no", and we will get to that in later sections of this book. The dog training markers can be powerful tools during the dog training because it can speed up the training process.

Then comes the challenge on how to let your dog learn the meaning of markers; well as far as my experience with many dogs has taught me, teaching the meanings of markers is one of the easiest thing you will ever teach your dog: just follow the particular procedure always, and you will be successful in 99 percent of the cases.

The process goes:

- Say the word that you want to use as a marker, like I mentioned "good" earlier.

- Follow the marker word by immediately giving your dog a treat as he performs the action.

- Repeat the marker when he is sitting.

- Repeat it when he is standing and so on and repeat it after every action.

- Repeat this process of using markers during daily training sessions every time, and as I mentioned in an earlier section, remain consistent.

Now the thing to understand is that there are different words used as markers, used at different times during the training. These marker words must remain and sound the same every time, and you should be very careful regarding any changes in your tone and pitch of voice while saying them. Don't let your mood for a particular situation change your tone or pitch to the extent that can get your dog confused. Now some of the marker words are listed as follows:

Reward Marker

As the name suggests, a reward marker is a word or sound used to mark the exact moment.

Our dog demonstrates a position like "sit" or a behavior that he has been given command about and he follows that command, the reward marker, such as "good," must be used immediately as he performs it. The reward marker can also be followed by a treat. The process must be repeated every time with the same word so that your dog can get conditioned to that very particular word.

The timing and consistency also matters here. Always give your dog the prize immediately as he follows your command. This will lead the dog to work in a friendlier environment. Use the same word every time and always follow with a small reward for the dog.

Correction Marker

A forbid marker is a word or sound that tells your dog to try something else. The action or behavior that they are doing is not exactly what you are looking for. Some common forbid markers are "stop" or "wrong" etc.

Once your dog knows what the marker words mean, then you can start to use them to provide feedback to your dog as you are teaching them about different cues (or commands). For example, if you are teaching your dog to come, you would say your dog's name, then the cue, "COME". If your dog moves towards you, you would use your positive marker, that can be a click of a clicker or "Good". If your dog does not move or moves away, you would say your negative marker, "Stop" or "Wrong".

Release Markers

Release words are those words through which your dog can know that he is done working. Generally, release words are used when you want your dog to come out of the position that you commanded him, such as if you asked your dog to sit. After some time, you can use a release word, so your dog can know that he can come out of that position. When you use a stay word, such as "sit-stay", the dog will stay in that position and then the release words are used to let your dog know that he can break out of that position and do whatever he wants to do until you give him the next command. Common release words are "Yes" or "Okay".

It is critical that there is a common language between you and your dog in order for you to teach your dog the behaviors you desire. And that is what the consistent and effective use of cues, markers, and release words give to you. Not only will you and your dog understand each other better, but your dog will learn new things faster and easier. Moreover, your bond with your dog will grow stronger than ever.

Secret #9: Praise Voice

What is the best thing you can do to respond to a good behavior by an animal or anything else? Well, in my consideration, the best way a person can respond to a good behavior is through a reciprocated good behavior. A word or two of praise not only can pay for the good behavior by someone else to you, but it does much more than that. It encourages the good doer to do it again and remain consistent with the good manners and behaviors.

Rewarding good behavior or mannerisms is not only necessary for the sake of further encouraging it but also for keeping the bad habits and unsuited behaviors at bay. Praising a person is much easier, as you can do so by just speaking some mere words of praise, kindness, and gratitude, but it can be a difficult job while dealing with dogs. Though dogs are much more intelligent and quicker learners than other animals of the pet category, it is basic understanding that you cannot just tell them in simple English or your native language that you are happy with them and their behavior is good and you want them to remain the same and avoid all the bad habits. You need more than that while dealing with dogs. So the term we use for dogs, instead of praise words, is **praise voice**. This is because they may not understand English, but they do understand pitch, tone, and certain words to which they are conditioned permanently due the training imparted to them.

By praise voice, we mean that, instead of relying on simple language and words for praising, we should be careful and cater to aspects like tone, pitch, and body language etc. while interacting with our dog. This is not something that is easy to master or be good at, and praise voice is probably one of the hardest things to get over for dog owners who happen to be male. It is where we have to get our voices in a high pitch, over the top, into an excitable baby voice, but the problem is it feels weird to many of the mature owners to do such weird and odd actions or speak or wail around the house in baby voices.

Then the problem is to know and master the pitch and tones correctly, which the dog will understand and conceive as something that is meant as praise for them or any particular behavior depicted by them, but once mastered and learned properly, the dogs will respond to that, and it can effectively be used as a reward other than treats or toys. Other than being an effective replacement for treats and toys etc., it also helps and improves the dog-owner relationship by leaps and bounds. Having an effective praise voice and being good at delivering it to your dog can greatly help you during training sessions with your dog. It is a means of communicating to your dog that you are happy with his behavior, and by using praise voice, you can communicate that you want him to keep this habit. Praise voice used in combination with friendly gestures and body actions that reflect your love and affection can greatly enhance its overall effects.

Praise voices are not just limited to cooing to your dog by making baby voices; rather, several of them exist. Another one of the most common examples of praise voice that exists with dog owners is the "good boy" phrase, said repeatedly in a friendly, soothing, and happy voice. As I said, combining a body action or a gesture of kindness or love, like rubbing his head or rubbing your dog's fur with your hands and fingers, while using the praise voices can very effectively deliver your message of felicitation to your dog.

Another aspect that we need to be very careful while using praise words is that our dogs know instantly the difference between praise that is really meant by us and the empty praises that we give to them just because we are supposed to but have no feeling behind it. Dogs are beings that understand emotions and sentiments in a way much better than most other pet animals, so this is why a lot of practice is required to master the art of using praise voice.

Talking about praise voice, it reminds me of the time when I was in military dog training academy. We actually did this again in the military as well, but here I would like to mention an aspect that the reader should be very careful about while using praise voice with their dog. We did not go all out with praise voice training on real dogs, but at first, we actually did this with ammo cans and stuffed animals. This practice gave us the cushion to make mistakes and learn from them and get really good at the praise voice art before actually implementing it on real dogs. In simpler words, we did this because we did not want to do it incorrectly on a real animal and be detrimental to the rest of our training if we were to stick with those dogs throughout the academy.

This practice helped us to get over the problem faced by us due to the hindrance of our mature habits and speech patterns. It helped us get over the shyness or the hesitation that we had in speaking or talking to our dogs in baby voices. Allocating so many resources and giving such importance to the aspect of correctly using praise voice in the military and carrying out days of rough practice on stuffed animals shows the level of significance that usage of correct praise voice holds in the field of dog training. This is especially important if a mature person is going to be dealing with a dog with the intention of effectively communicating with him.

Secret #10: No Means No

No means no, sit means sit, down means down. What I'm saying by this is: I say the command one time and only one time. If I have to say it three times in a row, the dog doesn't know that command and then it begins to not have the same effect. It then can also mean that the dog will respond whenever it feels like it wants to respond. If I'm saying, "Hey, Spot. Come. Come. Come." He will probably feel like my dad doesn't really mean to come until about the third time when he actually starts getting upset. No dog owners would like such a behavior in his or her dog, especially when we are out in some public place or when he is off leash and gets distracted by something like a car or chasing an animal through a busy street. Keeping this point in mind when we are training our dogs is of the utmost importance. We want to teach this and keep this in mind before we even start using correction. We want the dog to respond to a "No" and have the "No" mean something.

I usually want my "No" to be so effective that the dog will actually stop whatever it is doing, taking it as one of the "not allowed" things, so I don't have to give leash correction. I don't even put a collar. I don't use a leash. I don't use any such tools for my Dutch Shepherd, Vodnik. When he gets out of control, I give him one "No", and he responds to it immediately, quits whatever he is doing, looks back at me, and then comes back to a heel without me even saying anything. I don't give the command "heel". That's just what he has been conditioned to do after a while of practice, patience, consistency, structure, and my voice inflection. I am always in a happy, praising voice when I am giving him love, so when I tone it down and it is raspy and it is rough, and I give him that "No", it catches him off guard, and he knows I mean business.

Just like mentioned above in the example of Vodnik, it is important for your dog to know the meaning of the word that you have associated with the command. Like if you say the word no, the dog must know that whatever he is trying to do or is already doing is not right and he must stop that immediately or there will be consequences, like not getting his favorite treats or no playtime etc.

Just imagine a dog that is not really well-trained and likes everyone and everything around him. When you take him out on a walk with a loose leash attached to the collar and you do not have any control over him, it is really inappropriate. Imagine a dog pulling his owner with him because he wants to meet another dog that is coming from the other side of the road. This can lead to some kind of an accident, injuring both the dog and the owner. When two dogs owners come across each other, they must agree on their dogs meeting each other, or else there should be no communication of any kind. Taking the example of Vodnik, when I used to go out with him on a walk, I had trained him that he must ask for permission before meeting or greeting any other dog that passes by us during the walk. Whenever I interacted with a leashed dog owner on a walk, I used to ask him if it is okay for the two dogs to meet and only allowed Vodnik to meet the other dog if his owner agreed with me. I would use the word "greet" when I wanted him to meet with the other dog, and whenever I wanted Vodnik to ignore the other dog passing, I would use the words "pass by".

I have usually been against any type of greetings or meetings between two dogs who are both leashed because, when two dogs, meet they probably feel overjoyed and want to cuddle and twirl around, which leads to getting their leashes twisted with one another and causing a problem. Another reason I never liked Vodnik to meet other leashed dogs is because he may hurt himself by getting over excited. Whenever I wanted Vodnik to meet a dog, I would unleash him and tell him that he is not allowed to move away from me more than a few specific meters, which he followed very properly. And when I felt that it is enough, I would command Vodnik to come, and he would come to me right away. This is the perfect use of words that your dog listens to the command that you are giving him straight away, no matter how much he wants to stay there and play with the other dog. In simpler words, a command is a command, and it must be followed immediately.

Another important point to keep in mind when teaching your dog about the meaning of a certain word is that you must only say that word once, and the dog must follow the given command the first time. You must not repeat the word more than once for your dog to follow it. For example, by repeating a command three times, the dog will understand that he needs to follow it when it is repeated three times and will not follow that command if you say it only one time, or he may get the impression that he has the choice to ignore your commands whenever he likes.

In a nutshell, the word "no" means "no" and any of your commands mean immediate action is required.

Make sure your dog is well-aware of the "no" command and that he follows it when you only say it once because, many times, there will come situations where your single "no" command may even save your dog from a fatal incident or injury.

Section Four: Understanding the Nonverbals

When I was a young handler, I was so excited to work the dogs I felt like my whole job would be just sitting around playing fetch and just playing with a dog. Little did I know that there was science involved and learning theory to understand. It is hard to explain, but I honestly feel like I have a pretty good understanding of people, so I should have no problem working with a dog, giving them a couple belly rubs, a ball, some food and you have a best friend for life, right? Wrong, like I said, going through the Canine Academy in San Antonio is very much like going into a shelter and grabbing a canine partner. They have failed out of the selection process and now are training tools for new handlers, so they come with baggage and issues based on past experiences from other handlers or purely their own disposition.

I can remember when I had to work with the training dog Fflint (the two Fs were a sign that he was bred into the program, and so this is the only life he really knew). He was this gigantic muscled up Dutch Shepherd. If he was a person, he would be the gym rat, the meathead athlete. Just a beautiful specimen of a dog. Well, the first time I pulled him for obedience, I began to perform a phenomenon known as anthropomorphism, which is the attribution of human traits, emotions, or intentions to non-human entities. It is considered to be an innate tendency of human psychology. (We all do it to our dogs, i.e., oh my dog is jealous, or my dog is mad at me because I didn't give him a treat.) I did this by saying after only 45 mins of working with Fflint that he loves and respects me just because he let me pet him and take him on a walk. But I was not paying attention to the non verbals of the dog. He was wagging his tail, so I thought he was happy. He kept licking his lips, oh he just wants to give kisses. In all reality, I was young and blind to the fact that he was trying to say I was making him uncomfortable. I was overbearing and crowding him. I soon found out about non verbals the hard way when the obedience session was in full swing.

My point is, we all get so excited about meeting and interacting with the new dogs that we miss key moments when the dog communicates with us. This is extremely important any time we are dealing with fear- based, aggressive dog cases. We at Dogology University had a client with a Belgian Malinois, Nitro; they thought the dog was so cool, especially when they saw a police K9 demonstration for bite work. So, the husband purchased Nitro with the intent of making a personal protection dog. He introduced the dog to bite work at an extremely early age of about 7 weeks and started putting pressure on the dog by 9 weeks (meaning he backed tied the dog by itself and came towards it with whips to encourage a defensive drive). In my professional opinion, the problem is he was not watching the nonverbals. Nitro was probably telling him, hey bite work is fun, but now I am scared. So, Nitro bit in fear, and the husband stopped putting pressure on the dog. In that split second, Nitro associated, anytime I get scared, I bite and the thing that is causing my uncomfortableness will stop. So, when I got to meet Nitro, he walked in, licked his lips, and wagged his tail. I really pushed the boundaries, walked up to him and started petting him underneath his chin. When I walked away, he lunged and started barking and snapping at me. It became a game of habituation and the utilization of Hierarchy of Intensity, so that Nitro looked for guidance from his mom and dad instead of lashing out and biting strangers and other dogs.

Really though, Nitro's parents will never have the confidence to let him be left alone with strangers or play off leash at a dog park, and it could have been completely avoided if Nitro's dad had seen the non verbals at the early stages of training. Which brings me back to Fflint. I brought him out to do obedience, and the very first command was "SIT". With the military training method, if the dog does not do it, you give a correction with a choke chain in an upward movement paired with "NO", "SIT". Little did I know Fflint had been around the block for awhile. He heard sit, he braced for the correction, and as I gave the correction, Fflint came up leash trying to bite me. It was extremely scary but one of the best learning experiences I encountered, and I now pride myself on understanding the nonverbals of my dogs and my clients' dogs.

Not every non verbal section is as dramatic as these above, but they do illustrate the importance of utilizing and understanding these cues your dog gives you. Then we have the ability to talk to our dogs with hand signals and avoid any issues with generalization from our dogs with voice commands, which allows for an easier time teaching and training.

Secret #11: Avoidance Behavior

In avoidance, animals are naturally drawn to avoid situations that are deemed unsafe or that have a history of resulting in aversive, negative outcomes. The animal therefore feels relief when he's presented with an unpleasant situation and removes himself from that. Avoidance, in this case, involves negative reinforcement, meaning that the dog feels better when he avoids the situation and will feel compelled to avoid it as well in the future.

Avoidance behaviors are common in humans. If you are terrified of flying and on departure day you decide to cancel your flight because of your fear, you'll likely feel great relief. This relief will feel so good, the next time you must fly, you will feel tempted to avoid flying again. Same goes when there are people you don't like and you see this person at the mall. Most likely, you will walk in another direction and feel relief when you see this person hasn't noticed you. In animals, avoidance behavior is adaptive (linked to survival) to avoid situations that have a history of causing negative outcomes.

There are different times in a dog's life when he will be interested in getting involved in a situation one second and then trying to avoid that situation the very next second. In other words, the dog is trying to approach something at one moment because it feels very attractive, and then as he moves closer to the attractiveness, he will probably realize that there is some danger in that thing and will move backward. This process can even be repeated by the dogs again and again.

An example of this situation can be when you ask a stranger to feed your dog. The dog will first try to move towards him because the food in the stranger's hand is very much toothsome. As he moves forward towards that stranger, he will realize that, in his anticipation of the food, he just moved too close to the stranger, which can be dangerous for him. He will then probably move back towards the initial position. Then he may even move towards the stranger again, seeing and focusing on the delicious treat that he is going to get from that person. This can lead to confusion for your dog most of the time, so here I will suggest you feed your dog yourself, rather than handing over the food to some stranger and confusing your dog either to approach him or avoid him.

Another thing that should be kept in mind is that you should know about a dog's body language and know when he is approaching someone with pleasure and when he is trying to approach someone aggressively. An example of this can be taken when your dog approaches a friend of yours who is well-known to the dog and has come to your house for a very long time. The dog will try to reach him and try to get as close as he can to him so that they could meet properly. But when an unknown person tries to enter or enters your house through an inappropriate method, then the dog will probably try to reach him with an aggressive style and try to make the person run away. This also sums up all the avoidance behavior that is found among dogs. They might be trying to avoid one person at one time, and then at other time, they might be trying to approach some other person or the same person.

Now another example of a dog trying to avoid some sort of situation is when you mistakenly or unknowingly use a negative word with a positive command. You used a word with a negative command to prohibit your dog from doing a certain task in the past, and then you use the same word to make your dog follow a command. He will only end up in confusion, thinking that you are trying to make him avoid the task that you actually want him to perform. I mentioned in recent chapters how important it is for a dog trainer to have proper knowledge of the commands. The trainer must know the words to be used with the positive commands and the words to be used with negative commands and try his best not to mix up those words. If you mix up those words, the dog might even do the totally opposite thing of what you want him to do. It not only happens when you use a positive word with a negative command, but it can also happen vice versa. If you give a negative word with a positive command, then he might even try to avoid that situation, and when you give a positive word with a negative command, he will end up doing exactly what you did not want him to do.

It is very important for a trainer or a dog owner to know about the avoidance behavior signs. These signs include different behaviors like snarling, growling or barking, excessive licking, and even actually avoiding being touched, like getting up and moving to a different area. When a guest comes to your house and your dog has never seen him before or is not so familiar with that person, make sure to take care of the avoidance signs when introducing your dog to that person. Your dog may try to stay away from that person, turn and walk away or refuse to engage. These are signs that tell you that you should not force your dog to get engaged with the person who is a total stranger to him. And if you take your dog too close to the person, he might get scared and, in the end, may end up using his teeth to avoid that threat. There is no such thing in dogs not to bite someone or something that acts as a threat to them regardless of how trained and well-mannered they are.

Secret #12: A Wagging Tail Doesn't Mean A Happy Tail

The living beings of The Mighty Creator who dwell on this earth are as diverse in nature as they are in numbers. Millions and trillions of species inhabit this land, yet all of them have some distinct features or characteristics, making them distinct and identifiable individually from those certain traits that are identical to their specie. Science is what has helped us make progress in understanding this world and the secrets of our fellow inhabitants of this planet more than anything ever could have. We progressed from the stone age and hunting for food to the developed era of present day and the science of farming for food needs and understanding animals and their behaviors in millions of aspects. A prime example of this exemplary progress is dogs. Dogs are the species whose utilization started from mere animals to pets and then to thousands of applications nowadays from guide dogs to therapy dogs, from sniffing ones to guard dogs or herding dogs. This vast range of utilization in such a wide variety of different fields and contrasting environments proves the versatility of the dogs and their behavioral sciences.

We may have come a long way from the very start, but there are a lot of miles to go in this field. Progress has not stopped and is on its way forward. Research and science are always providing new information that allows us to interpret the behaviors of dogs, and not just that, but it is also helpful to us in re-interpreting the behaviors that we thought we understood very well. A mere simple gesture that we just took as a simple act of behavioral signature of sadness or anger may have much deeper meanings, and our dog may be trying to say much more than what we interpret out of those simple actions.

A prime example of such behavioral characteristic is the meaning of a dog's tail wagging.

This is perhaps the most common misinterpretation of a dog's behavioral characteristic. There exists this commonly acknowledged and believed myth that a dog wagging it's tail is happy and friendly and a wagging tail means all the right signs of a good and joyous mood. Well, there is no complete denying that fact as well. It is common that some wags are indeed associated with happiness and a good felicitous mood, but then comes the new studies and surveys on several dogs that suggest there can be more to a seemingly simple and friendly suggesting action or gesture. Some studies have suggested such behavior can be associated with certain psychological problems like fear, insecurity, a social challenge, or even a warning that if you approach, you are apt to be bitten!

The real challenge starts after a new behavior is dug out or a behavioral characteristic and its associations are discovered. Surely, we cannot just sit there and expect dogs to go by our expectations all the time. They are a diverse species and the same action means one thing in one being and the very same action or gesture could mean something totally opposite to the next. The solution starts, as my previous sections have explained, with patience, determination, and more importantly a grown up and mature approach, involving no haste in judging your dog and his behavioral signatures as being similar to others. This may be recommended for many other cases and scenarios of life, but it especially applies to dealing with dogs, and it is to have the belief in your heart that every dog is a distinct being, and he is supposed to be different from other ones, ranging from mere slight differences to huge variations and contrasts when compared to each other. This requires patience as well as knowledge. And then you need a lot of determination, reaching to the depth of understanding your dog's behavioral signs. Never expect random things from your dogs or expect your dog to behave or react in a certain way to any of your commands or gestures because you have seen other dogs respond in a similar fashion on a YouTube channel or in the park. Be mentally and emotionally ready to accept the differences and distinctions of your dog from others.

Then comes the learning part; don't just expect things from your dog. Randomly, always observe your dog keenly whenever you are with him/her and whenever you are not (which can be done by some innovative improvisations and untraditional ways). Observe how he responds to certain actions or events occurring in his surroundings, and then go for your research, developing a hypothesis, making a concept in your mind of your dog's behavioral patterns. Observe, especially regarding the behaviors that may seem to you that your dog has in contrast to other ones and then start digging in. Keep going until you don't trace it back to some solid reason or logic behind the particular distinctive behavioral pattern and then the step of finding solutions starts. Always remember this: "The deeper you cut the roots, the more effectively you eradicate a problem."

When trying to effect change, you can instead of trying to change your dog by force, try amending yourself and your methodologies involved with him, and when you would do so, you will find it easier then and you will find your dog making progress faster this way. Then always be ready to change your ways and procedures if one is not working out; accept the versatility and try to dissolve yourself into the situation, instead of trying to make a lesser intelligent being cope with your comprehension and cognitive levels. This is what will make you successful in achieving great goals with your dog and developing a better understanding for each other and relieving you of many potential hardships.

Secret #13: Teaching Hand Signals

Hand signals can be used to train a dog, and it's just as easy to do as verbal commands. Essentially, it's sign language; you'll use your hands to signal to your dog what you want it to do, such as sit, down, come, or heel. Dogs are excellent at reading body language. Many even find it much easier to read what people are saying with their bodies than with spoken language.

Hand signals are useful in a variety of situations. For instance, they're often easier to use or required for competitive obedience. Deaf dogs obviously won't be able to respond to spoken commands, so hand signals allow their owners to train them just like any other dog. And, if you enjoy training, this is one more thing to add to your dog's repertoire of skills. Just think how impressed your friends will be when you have your dog doing all sorts of tricks with just a few small movements of your hand.

Some commands that you can train to your dog to follow through your hand signals are sit, stand, heel, and more. There are many signs that can be used for each command, but the thing to remember when teaching your dog sign language is that you make sure you do not mix up the signs. Only use a single sign with a single command, and then do not use the same sign with any other command and do not use another sign with the same command because it will only lead your dog to confusion. The simpler and shorter you keep your signs, the easier it will be for your dog to understand and learn those signs.

Now, the sign that you can use for your dog to go to sit position is easy and simple. When you give the sit command to your dog, just try moving your open hand completely from top towards the bottom, only moving it a few inches. When the dog sees that your hand came from the top towards the bottom, i.e, from a high place to low place, the dog will understand that he also needs to get low, following the movement of the hand. Now if you are teaching a deaf dog, it will be easy for him to understand the movement of your hand. He'll be able to follow your hand and go to the sit position, from the top towards the bottom just like the movement of your hand.

Similarly, you can give the stand command to your dog using the sign language and a sign that is just like the one used for the sit command, but it will be opposite from that. When you give the stand command to your dog, move your hand from the bottom towards the top, from a lower position to a higher position. This will allow your dog to understand that he needs to go to a higher position then from his current position just like the movement of your hand. The smoother you move your hand and the simpler the sign you choose, the easier it will be for the dog to follow your command without even listening to it.

If you are giving your dog the command to stop or stay, you can use a hand sign, keeping your hand vertical and still. This sign shows no movement in your hand, meaning that the dog should stop any kind of movement that he is doing at that moment and stay at a certain position, depending on the given commands.

An important sign that you need to remember is the watch me sign. Choose a watch me sign according to your way and then teach it to your dog before teaching him anything else. It is the first and the most necessary thing in sign language training; your dog is looking towards you and has no concentration on anything except your hand. Choose a hand through which you will give the command and then always remember to use the exact same hand every time.

After your dog understands the watch me sign and is able to follow it properly and put all his focus towards you after the command, the next thing that comes is that you choose a command and the sign that you will choose for that command. Always pick short and easy signs to make it easier and simpler for the dog to understand them. After your dog understands that command properly, then move to the next command and repeat the same procedure as the previous command using a different sign for a different command. Try using signs that are distinct from one other in every meaning, so that your dog does not end up getting confused which command to follow and which not to follow.

You can use voice command in the beginning of teaching your dog sign language. But as the training proceeds and your dog gets a better understanding of the hand commands and the sign language while given with the voice commands, stop giving the voice commands and try to make your dog follow the signs without saying anything. This will increase your dog's efficiency to follow the sign language to a greater extent.

When beginning training, keep a small treat in your hand to give to the dog after he listens to your command. And do it again and again using the treat. A treat in your hand will make the dog more interested in following the motion of your other hand because he will be desperately waiting to have that treat. Then get rid of the treat when you give the command or the hand signal and give your dog the treat after he follows the given sign or command.

Practice sign language more often with your dog indoors and outdoors because it will make him more efficient in following the commands and practice is going to make it quicker and easier for the dog to follow your commands.

Section Five: Important Commands to Train

When I take my dog, Vodnik, to the dog park, he is completely off leash. I notice other owners have their dogs off leash, too, but when it is time to go, they are constantly chasing other dogs. They are constantly avoiding the owners, and the owners actually have to get up and start running towards their dogs to pick them up by the collar to get them out. We also have a neighbor right down the street from us who has a little Yorkie. The Yorkie would literally run out the front door, and the owner spends at least 30 to 45 minutes trying to collar the dog and get it to come back. I feel like heeling is a very important command to teach.

When I was in Canine Academy, I had a dog named Kodi. I would have to take Kodi out to the bathroom hill, and I would have to put her on a dual-collar, which is the choke chain and the flat collar, and then only I could take her for a walk. The entire time, she would be pulling around the hill and just dragging me around behind her. I would have to wrap the leash around my right and left hands and try to position the weight of her strength equally on my hands, but after a while, I started developing calluses on the webbing of my fingers. It was something I did not look forward to every day that I had to pull her. It is inconvenient, unpleasant, a workout to get your dog out for a walk. But, when your dog understands heel, you can actually walk your dog with the ease of just holding the leash with a finger.

It is very important that you teach your dog the heel command. When you take your dog out for a walk and he has learned the heel command, you do not need to chase your dog for miles when he runs off. All you will need is to give him the heel command, and he will come right beside you and stay there until you allow him to go somewhere. The heel command also comes in handy at other times, for example when you are out with your dog for your dog to meet new dogs; he would not run away behind other dogs, and you would not need to chase him through the streets.

Secret #14: Come

Come is probably one of the most important commands for me, because I know that dogs can escape. I don't want them to run too far ahead of me. I don't want them to go chasing after cars. When I say come, I want the dog to return to me and stand looking directly at me. I also understand that people are still going to use retractable leashes, even though I personally hate them. I know that retractable leashes break, and what do you do at that point? You have to get them under control. You don't want an unknown dog to attack your dog, nor would you want your dog to run into traffic and have an accident with something, taking a risk with his life as well as others'.

I also have seen dogs chase squirrels. No matter if you have a six foot fence, a five foot fence, or if the squirrel comes by and is taunting your dog, which as dog owners we all know can occasionally happen, our dog will get a full head of steam and can clear fences with ease. Just imagine your dog in a situation chasing a squirrel on a road and a vehicle is coming closer and closer to him. Yet, your dog is still unaware of the circumstances chasing that squirrel. You yell "Come". What will your dog do? Will he stop chasing the squirrel and immediately reach back to you, realizing the danger he is in? Or will he just go on chasing the squirrel, making a great mistake that will possibly lead to an accident? Believe me you do not want to wait for this situation to happen to find out the answer.

This all depends on a simple point that, had you given him the proper training to come when you say "Come", it could have been avoided. I hope your dog never gets into that kind of situation, but still he must know that "Come" means to stop any other thing that he is doing and come back to you. Having no equipment, but having our dogs obedient to "Come" can come in handy in real life situations.

The next important thing in dog training is that you must have clear meaning of the commands that you are giving to your dog. Make sure that you do not mix up commands. The positive commands are different, and the negative commands must be different. If you are trying to teach your dog a positive command, but you have used that word before with a negative command, then your dog will have a hard time understanding what you are trying to tell him. Because when you give him the command to perform a task, he will only imagine that you are trying to forbid him from the task that he is doing at the current moment.

This only makes the training harder for both you and your dog.

The next thing that comes after the correct use of words is that your dog must be able to listen and follow to your commands, regardless of the distractions around him. You must train him properly to listen and follow your commands, regardless of the surroundings. This can come in handy a lot of times in life. Your dog will also be able to follow to your commands in a place where other dogs just do not listen to their owners. You must train your dog well for this purpose, starting from a place with minimal diversions and then moving to more and more distracting surroundings.

Remember that training your dog is a slow process and requires patience. The more patience you have, the better the results of your training, and your dog will get more time to learn and practice the commands.

For the training of any new command to your dog, the first thing that you need is a good relationship between you and your dog. And after your dog follows the given command, he must be given a small treat for encouragement. Remember, when you are trying to teach a new command to a dog, you can call that command combined with the dog's name. For example, suppose my dog's name is Vodnik. I can teach a new command to him, like "Vodnik come" or "Vodnik stand" etc. But the thing to remember here is that you must use the name either only for positive commands or negative commands. For example, if I recently used Vodnik's name to hinder him from a task that he is performing, he will know that, whenever his name is called, he must halt anything that he is doing at that moment. Now if I say "Vodnik come" or some other positive command, he may not be able to perform the desired task based on the recent training that I have been giving him in which I associated his name with one or more negative tasks.

The same thing goes for the word that you pick for the command. Suppose if you had used the word "Come" while punishing your dog or scolding him, then he will likely try to avoid the task that you are telling him to do because you scolded him using the same word. I suggest that you choose a word that has not been used for him or has been positively used before.

The next thing that you must take care about is that you must never do any action after the dog follows your "come" command that will make him think twice before following the same command again next time. For example, if you told your dog to come, which he did, and after that you scolded him because of some mistake, it will only make him less willing to follow that command next time. Remember to give a little treat to your dog after he performs the desired task properly because it will please him, and he will be even more excited and quick in following that command next time.

Remember one last thing; when your dog has mastered the "come" command, it does not mean that he is done. The command must be repeated daily so that your dog can perform that command with quick reflexes and sharpness when it's needed the most. Come command can come in handy most of the time in real life situations.

Secret #15: Heel

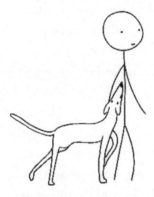

The heel command means that a dog must stay with you and walk right beside you, not ahead of you and not lagging behind you either. The dog must keep up the same pace with you and walk with you.

One of the first clients I ever had was a Bernese mountain dog, named Diesel. Diesel always wore a harness, and Diesel was a destructive chewer. Diesel kept chewing on his harness and eventually just pulled through the harness, broke it and was off to the races. I had to chase him for about two and a half miles until he was done running, but I was exhausted. I dreaded when I had to go walk Diesel by myself. I would try to bring someone with me. It was always a hassle, always a pain, and not enjoyable. When Diesel was just a client for dog walking, I eventually took it upon myself to teach Diesel to heel. Later, I found out that the owners started taking him for a walk and noticed a dramatic difference in Diesel's attitude towards walking, and they actually began to enjoy walking and spending more time with Diesel.

The owners did relay to me that they thought the harness was more useful for walking Diesel, but what this does is actually encourages pulling behavior. In the military, we use the harnesses to teach independence or to encourage independent behavior when searching roadways in Iraq for explosives. We don't want to be on top of the dog. We want to give the dog the ability to work independently of us to help alleviate some of the casualties that were happening with improvised explosives and pressure plates. If we are using these on the military working dogs, what will that do for your high energy house dog? It's going to encourage that independent behavior. It is going to encourage and compound the issue of pulling when you are taking it for a walk.

What tool do I use to teach heel? It is going to be the prong collar. I know a lot of people are hesitant about the prong collar. It looks very, very nasty, harsh. Just an unkind, unpleasant tool, but it is probably the best tool to use because the prongs go evenly around the dog's neck so that, when the pressure is applied, it's applied in a fashion that does not cause much pain. It just causes discomfort. Then, it deters the dog from pulling and other things. It is more humane than the choke chain, which can be applied incorrectly and accidently put on backwards or sized wrong, which can cause a lot of medical issues as well. The only time that I recommend using a harness is if your dog is diagnosed with a health condition with their throat or esophagus, but besides that, the prong collar is the way to go for teaching heel.

Now coming back to the point of training your dog to heel, the question is how you realize the need for training heel. You realize the need for reaching heel when you go for a walk and your dog runs too far ahead when you unleash him and you have to run and chase him until he is done running or you are exhausted. When you are training your dog to heel, it is a must that you take him for a walk on a daily basis and teach him to stay not ahead or behind but right beside you. I know it is hard to go for a walk on a daily basis because everyone has a busy schedule, and this task becomes even harder in the beginning because your dog just runs too far ahead of you and you have to go chase him so that he does not get into any trouble, like a car accident or getting involved in a fight with some homeless dog. Sometimes your dog may stay behind because he is not interested in having a walk on that day. This means that your dog really needs heel training. When you teach your dog the heel command, it means that he must maintain the pace with you, whether you are walking really slow or a bit faster than your regular walking speed. The heel command also makes your dog realize that you are the one with the control here, and he must follow as you say without any delay.

Your dog must be aware of the heel command if you ever wish to go on a walk without your dog leashed and want it to finish peacefully without any critical situation taking place. Even when your dog is on a leash, heel makes it even easier to go on a walk with him as he would not be applying any pressure against the leash to go faster or run ahead of you, and with your dog aware of the heel command, you will not have to go chase him and exhaust yourself.

The heel training must begin in small places like your living room or a fenced backyard so your dog will not be able to run away from you, and you will not have to chase him. Command your dog to sit in a place and then start moving towards the forward direction slowly and tell your dog to come with you using the heel command word like "follow" or "heel". Then after he follows the given command properly, always have a small piece of treat for him. Repeat this exercise regularly, always ending with a small treat. After a few days when your dog has learned the basics of the heel command, take him for a walk and then train him with a leash on for a few days in an open area, and after that, try training your dog without a leash. This way, he will slowly learn to heel, and you will enjoy going out on walks with him.

Remember that, during the training, your dog must be totally focused on the commands that you are giving him. If you are somewhere where you feel that your dog is being distracted from the training, try to remove the distraction and start the training again. The second thing to remember here is a common thing while training any kind of command to your dog, and it is to follow a successful action with a treat.

Secret #16: Proper Introduction

Back in the colonial days, when a man would greet a woman, the woman would curtsy. The man would kiss the woman's hand, just showing good, proper manners and giving a sign of good upbringing and belonging to a respectable family. That is what we should be thinking of with our dogs when introducing them to new people, other dogs, and even babies. I run into a lot of people who say their dog is not aggressive, or it is completely trained, but you also see these same people completely repeating themselves, "Come, come, come." Or, the dog is chasing the neighbor's dog up and down the fence, barking like anything and is not listening or behaving when they are excited about something. This is not always a sign of aggression, but it is a built-up defensive drive that it cannot relieve its stimulation, and it is going to chase this other dog continually. If it can't ever actually be introduced, it is going to be so built up, so overzealous that the other dog will not know how to react. It is doomed and not advantageous for a proper introduction.

We also have to keep in mind that, if our dog has shown defensive or aggressive tendencies, we can't allow those feelings to cloud our judgment. We need to be aware and cognizant of this fact, but we can't keep the leash tight because that tightness that you are feeling will travel down the leash and make the dog uneasy, and again, will make the dog lash out because of it.

Now there are different situations in our daily lives where dogs can show a variety of behaviors, ranging from being very aggressive or being very defensive at times and then at times showing behavior of reclining to a corner or a nook of the house and staying there, unwilling to come out. We need to know how to control our dog in such moments. If you think that you will keep a medium length leash around your dog and stretch it whenever the dog gets aggressive, you are wrong. When you have a leash around an aggressive dog, you will have a hard time holding him back from running behind other dogs or barking at them. If your dog is healthy and strong, there are chances that he may even take you dragging behind himself if you hold the leash when he is getting very aggressive. That leash can also become a problem for others when the dogs get aggressive. It might get stuck or wrapped around someone's legs or feet if they are in the path, and your dog could drag them, resulting in possible major injuries or be fatal.

The question here is, if you cannot leash your dog, then what is the way to stop him from chasing other dogs or barking at them? You cannot expect a dog not to bark at all at other dogs, but with properly trained and practiced commands, you might be able to prevent your dog from running behind other dogs and running into a possible accident. When your dog is properly trained and you have proper command over him, you do not even need a leash to go out with him. He will not perform any task without your permission.

Now the training includes letting your dog know how to meet other dogs. He must be trained to meet other dogs only when you allow him and trained enough to chase something with your permission only. Back when I had Vodnik, he was trained to meet other dogs only when I allowed him. We would find other dogs on the sidewalk; I would talk with the owner and only then allow Vodnik to meet the dog. Vodnik knew that he cannot stay here for a long time and will have to leave upon my call, so he never got so attached with the other unknown dogs. I used to unleash Vodnik when he met another dog. You should only do this if you know that your dog is trained enough to come back on your single call. Otherwise, this meeting may end in you pulling the two dogs apart from one another or you trying to get your dog under leash again, holding him by his collar. Vodnik would come back to me on my single call when I called him.

It is important to unleash your dog because, when they meet, they may hop around here and there and end up getting their leashes tangled. Tangled lashes can be so hard to separate, and sometimes, it can be dangerous for one dog who is less healthy. The healthier dog may start to run, dragging the other dog with him, even when the dog does not want to keep up, resulting in fatal injuries for the dog. This is the main reason I always advised dog trainers to unleash the dogs. But I also told them to remember that they can only unleash their dog when they know their dog is trained and mature enough to come back to you from his new buddy when you call.

It is an important thing that the dogs know how to meet other people too. If your dog barks at everyone who sets foot in your house, it is probably wrong because some people not as close to you may get scared and avoid coming to your house next time. He must know when he needs to bark and at what time he must stay silent. One thing that a dog must understand is the right way for people to enter the house and the wrong way. He must know he has permission to bark when someone tries to enter the house in a wrong way. But he must not bark at people who come to the house with you or through the entrance in a proper way.

Section Six: Practice for Perfection

I am sure you have heard the phrase: "practice makes perfect!" Well, this is especially applicable to the scenario of keeping dogs and then training them for a certain thing. Whatever you are trying to teach your dog, if you don't practice enough, you will never be able to gain your desired results, no matter what unique or efficient way or method you choose to train your dog. Training a dog is one thing where enough practice would surely pay off, and the more you practice, the better results you can achieve.

Relating this back to the time when I was in the military and used to deal with dogs there and train them for certain commands and routines, no matter how many times we would train, no matter how many times we would practice, even when we could hit 99% of our odor for detection, and even after we succeeded in finding every decoy and fulfilling almost all the goals, the times I would think that Kato And I have become the perfect training partners, , the military would still send us for pre-deployment training anyway. At times, this could be frustrating to me as to why we still have to go for more training when we are already almost perfect, but the military has its own ways of doing things and achieving goals and all that was designed after careful behavioral studies and statistics that I didn't know much about at the time. But every time I practiced more with Kato, I would see improvement in Kato's behavior and conduct, and every time, I learned a few new things as well. This is what convinced me of the importance of continuing to practice always no matter how good and trained or groomed your dog has become.

You see, the fact is that we could have low expectations from a dog, but dogs are intelligent creatures, and they tend to surprise you every time you go out with them for a training session with their quick learning and grasping of new things and environments and understanding those which are familiar to them in better and more enhanced ways, which at times, we are not expecting them to learn.

Coming back to my military training session with Kato and pre- deployment sessions, pre-deployment training is just practice for us to go down range to the Middle East and be deployed. We would practice movements. We would practice more with detection. We would practice roadway clearings, buried aids, mass odors, but we needed to practice every variable possible. Just like football players, like the Patriots, Bill Belichick, they practice the two minute drill. They practice quick change drills. They practice goal line stances. The idea is that they want to make sure to have every variable covered that could possibly happen during a game, just like we would practice for deployments. We just wanted to make sure that anything could happen at any time, we would be prepared for it by virtue of our practice.

We want you guys to do the exact same thing. This is called proofing, and there are three disciplines to proofing to ensure that our dog has been proofed for the commands. Everything in this world which you want to master requires a lot of practice. The ninjas are masters in using a sword, but they still practice using their sword sixteen hours every day, which makes them professionals in what they are doing. That is exactly what you need to do with your dog too. Now I am not saying that you need to train your dog sixteen hours a day; of course, that will be too exhausting for your dog. When your dog learns a command and you move on to a new command, make sure that you do not forget to train the command that you recently taught your dog.

When you are training him for a new task, practice the old trained commands at the same time. This will make sure that your dog does not forget all the valuable lessons that you have been giving to him. Practice is consistency. The more you practice the taught commands with your dog, the easier and quicker for your dog to follow them.

Even after you have finished training, make sure that you do a rehearsal on a daily basis.

The only secret behind the success of so many dog trainers while training their dogs is that they do a lot of practice of the commands that they are teaching them. More and more practice would condition the dog and its mental levels and cognitive receptors of a certain command on which and when it is done so. Whenever that command is given to him, his body would automatically start to perform the task that the command requires him to do. Another aspect to practicing is that it makes the reflexes of your dog quicker to that command, reducing the reaction time a lot.

As I mentioned earlier as well, while practicing, you should always keep in mind the limits of your dog and then train him accordingly. If you just try to train and enforce into his mind more than he could learn in a single day, then he will end up learning only a small part of everything, instead of learning a single command properly. Teaching your dog commands one by one will consume a lot of time, but it is the most convenient and easy way for you and your dog.

The time taken by the dog to learn a specific command depends on your dog and its breed as well. But the more practice you do, the more familiar your dog becomes with the surroundings and the tasks that he needs to be performing on a daily basis. The dog must know the proper meaning of the words that you are using with the commands to tell him what it actually means and what do you really want him to do.

Like the old saying "slow and steady wins the race", you need to make progress at a slow speed, making sure that your dog is learning the stuff you are teaching him. If you are making progress continuously and on a daily basis, then it is still good no matter how slow.

Secret #17: Duration

As I said before, there are three D's to proofing. The first D is duration. Duration is the amount of time that we allow the dog into that command. This will build up the dog for an automatic stay, so we don't always have to constantly say stay, but if we do, the dog knows that we are asking it to stay in this position. I have taught Vodnik to sit and stay before we drop his meal. I don't want Vodnik jumping up and knocking the bowl out of my hand. I don't want him, before I even get the bowl down, to have his nose in the food bowl and scarfing it down his throat. I want him to be controlled because this will help with him eating and avoiding incidents, like eating too quickly and possibly getting bloated. I also would do this with Kato. We would sit and wait to make sure that he was actually in odor, and we would drop his reward. Again, the secret here is not to wait too long.

When the training is in the beginning process, the owner must sit close to the dog's head while he is in sit position and give him the treat as soon as he follows your given command while staying near him so that he can feel more relaxed. Give a small treat to your dog while he is still in the sit position and again after a short interval of time. If your dog breaks the sit position and stands, then you must stop giving him the treat and wait and see if he goes back to the sit position or not. If he goes to the sit position, then it is good, and you must continue the training as you were doing before, and if he does not go back to the sit position himself, craving the treat from your hand and you have to give him the sit command once again to make him sit, then you should begin the training once again, and this time try to increase the duration of sit command.

As the training moves on and your dog becomes more familiar with the position that you are trying to teach him, you can increase the duration of that position and increase the time interval between the treats that you give to your dog during the training. Suppose you gave your dog a treat after every 10 seconds when you started training him; now take that time interval to like 20 seconds. As the training progresses forward, keep increasing the time interval of your commands and keep reinforcing them during the training.

Gradually, you must also learn to stand up, commanding your dog to stay in sit position or whatever position you commanded him to stay in. Bend down a little bit to give the treat and then stand up straight. This is probably one of the most difficult points in the dog training, and most new dog trainers do not know about the time intervals that they must maintain in giving a treat to the dog they are training and end up giving a lot of treats to the dog, which will probably make him less comfortable and harder to continue the training.

At this point, it must always be kept in mind that we should not give the dog a lot of treats with small intervals of time for just staying in a certain position.

This will probably ruin your dog's habit of hard work, and he will just be imagining that he will get a treat even if he does not do anything but just stay in a certain position, which is not good by any means in dog training.

As the training progresses, regularly continue to increase the time intervals between each treat given. Remember that, if your dog breaks the position that he was supposed to be in, then you must begin the training once again, giving him the sit and stay command or whatever positions you would like him to stay in. Also increase the duration of the time for which the dog needs to stay in a certain position as the training progresses forward. Try to realize that, if your dog is getting more comfortable in a certain position, like transferring his weight to one side and loosening the legs, he is now feeling relaxed in that position. This will help your dog to be more obedient, and you will have full control over him whenever you go out in public etc.

Remember to learn about the dog's body language and notice his movements when he is in a certain position according to your command. He might be feeling very tired of a certain position and probably would like to break out of that position if he has been there for a long time. As a trainer, it is vital to note the body language of the dog and know what that body language actually means. If your dog is really tired of the position, then you must allow him to break the position before he breaks the position himself without your consent because he is tired of it. If he breaks the position without your permission and you scold him in a harsh manner, then he might get afraid of breaking that position, which will eventually lead to a point where your dog will actually try not going into that position so that he does not have to break it again, ruining the primary purpose of the command. That is why it is very important for a trainer to know about the dog's body language and know when your dog has reached its limit. When you feel that he has reached the limit, you must allow him to come out of that position and give him a little extra treat so that he feels more excited and encouraged when he is in that position next time. This explains why duration knowledge is very important when training your dog.

Secret #18: Distance

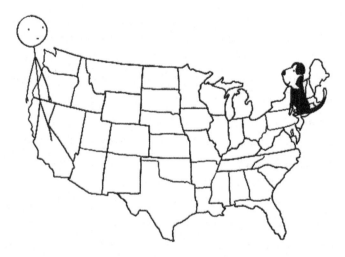

Distance is the second "D" in the principles for proofing. This is the distance between me and the dog. It's important if eventually we want to teach our dog off leash obedience. We can't always have the dog on a three foot leash or a six foot leash, but we can get him on 16 foot, 36 and 360 leashes and continue to work on the commands until we're comfortable enough to drop a leash and start working off leash.

I recently had a photo shoot and we worked with a couple of current and past clients. We were able to put six dogs in the down position and walk away. They made a beautiful U. I was able to come forward and look at the camera. All the dogs were away from me, away from each other, and they knew that the distance did not matter. The duration did not matter. Eventually, we would reward them.

When can your dog be ready to understand your cues from a far distance? To teach your dog to understand and follow your commands regardless of the distance between you and him, you must move to a place with the least distractions, so that the dog can concentrate more effectively on the commands you are giving him. The fewer the distractions, the quicker your dog will progress as he will only need to follow the commands that you are giving him, and there will be no other distractions.

Now in the beginning, the trainer (you) must understand that you must stand near the dog just like usual training that you give him. Then command your dog to sit and stay. After that, you must start moving backwards slowly and then give any other command like while standing or in prone position from some distance. At first, many times, your dog will be unable to follow your command, as he will be more focused on the command you gave him before starting to step back, and he will be distracted a little bit at the start by your movements. Remember that, when the training is in the beginning, the distance does not need to be in feet, but it should be a few inches between you and your dog. And as the training progresses and your dog starts to understand and follow your commands from that distance, then move a few more inches backward and then command him from that distance. The distance must be increased from inches to feet slowly as the training progresses further.

Now a big mistake that is done by a lot of new trainers while teaching this command to their dog is that they add too much distance between themselves and the dog, especially in a distracting environment.

This is why I recommended above using a place with the least distractions as that will help you a lot. If you add a large distance in the very beginning of the training, then you must not expect your dog to learn the commands quickly as that will be hard for him to understand from a longer distance than usual. Start from a smaller distance and then gradually raise your criteria as the training progresses further and your dog becomes ready for it. You must keep your expectations low in the beginning. If you keep the expectations too high in the very beginning and your dog is unable to come up to that level, then you should understand that you need to lower the expectations right now and raise them later when your dog is ready. If your dog is not performing as per the desired results even after a passage of time, then you must realize that you are making some mistake, and you must figure that out as soon as possible.

It may be hard for some of you to understand the concept that I am trying to give here because it is really hard to give your dog training this slowly, increasing the distance between him and you gradually with time, and I know it is very time consuming. But the point behind this concept is that your dog will be able to perform more efficiently and will remember your training even after months or years as he learned that slowly and with full attention towards only one thing.

The training of your dog is a lifetime process, and it is very hard to keep it up in a well-mannered fashion, but by following the process mentioned and keeping track of your activity, gradually with time, you will create a higher level of understanding between you and your dog that will help you in training him in this command and further commands that you are going to teach him.

Benefits of Obedience from a Great Distance

What are the benefits of teaching your dog to follow your commands from a greater distance, and why you should spend so much time teaching him this? There are many benefits that may come handy in real life situations.

Imagine if you go on a walk with your dog and he is chasing a squirrel off-leash and there are chances that he might bump into something or someone. You can use the come or stop command from where you are standing to call him back to you. Now you did not needed to run behind him to give him a command but just gave it from a farther distance, and he still followed it because he has been trained by you to follow the commands given to him, regardless of the distance between you two. This is the benefit of giving him all the training, and this is the fruit of your hard work that now saves your dog from any kind of accident and saves the energy that you would have wasted running behind him.

Secret #19: Distractions

Again, at the photo shoot that I mentioned earlier leaves were falling, there were other dogs around, there were other people around, there were kids throwing leaves and doing other stuff. We were at a park. It was crazy distracting, even for me, but distractions are an important component of proofing. If the dogs don't break position during distractions, during distance, and they can do it for a while, that means they have been proofed; they have been practicing, and you can be confident that no matter what is going on, you can ask for a command and the dogs will act to it immediately. You don't have to rely on a food reward. You don't have to rely on a clicker. You don't have to rely on an E-Collar. You can just rely on your voice, because that is always readily available.

Now the question that arises here...is that how to train your dog for listening and performing whatever command you have given him, regardless of any surroundings and distractions?

Well, an easy way one can create distractions for a dog at a small level to begin his training is by changing the environment of the surroundings in which you are training your dog. Regular change of the environment will act as a distraction for your dog. When you change the surroundings of the training, then remember you must be a bit on the beginner level of your training because your dog is in these new surroundings, and he will take some time in listening and responding to your commands. You can also make the training in new surroundings easier for yourself and more comfortable for the dog by increasing the amount of the treat that you give to your dog when he follows a certain command that you gave him. This will encourage him to work in the new conditions, making the training easier.

Now we want our dog to respond to our commands instantly without any delay, regardless of the circumstances and environment in our surroundings. A simple way to begin the training for this is by moving your dog from room to room in your house, which will probably act as a change in the surrounding as you change rooms. You must realize in which room your dog feels the most uncomfortable and most distracted and begin training him slowly from other rooms and then leading him into the room in which he felt most distracted when you gave him a walk through all the rooms. Now the point to notice is that, if you immediately take your dog to the room where he felt the most distracted, then he will be unable to focus on your commands, and most of the focus will be on the distractions, which will lead to the point that your dog will not be able to follow the commands that he has been taught because he is too distracted.

When you change the rooms from least distracting to most distracting slowly and in a gradual fashion, then it will be easier for your dog to work. When your dog works in an environment with few distractions and then comes to a place with a higher level of distraction, he would not feel as distracted as he would have if you directly brought him into the room that distracted him the most. Now remember that your dog is working in a new environment and surrounded with distractions, and he will not be able to perform at the same level at which he used to perform when there were no distractions. The trainer must realize this key aspect of distraction training and go a little bit lighter on the training than the regular training.

Another way you can keep your dog involved and interested in working and training with you in an environment with distractions is by increasing the amount of the treats you use to give him when he performs in an environment with no distractions. It is probably harder for the dogs to work in an environment with a lot of distractions because, just like a human brain, their brain also focuses on everything that is going on in the surroundings, making it difficult to perform the task in hand. The same also happens with us in our daily life.

When your dog starts to train properly and listen to and perform every command that you give him properly in every room, it is time to move outside. Go for your backyard or your garage, i.e., where the distractions are higher than the rooms but less than a busy street. Now remember, as you move from rooms to the backyard or garage of your house, the level of the distractions will be increased, reducing the efficiency by which your dog listens and perform to your commands. He may take a bit longer than he took in the beginning when you started training him in the least distracting room, but remember that, in those rooms, the distractions were fewer, and here in the courtyard, the number of distractions has increased. Many distractions are added to the environment in which you are training your dog when you move from the rooms to the courtyard, like noises from outside, smells of other animals roaming around your backyard or on the nearby streets, temperature of the surroundings etc. Do not worry if you have to start the training your dog in distractions again from step one and just do it like you did in the rooms. Go polite on the dog and increase the amount of treats you give to your dog when he performs the desired task in the backyard than you gave him when back in the rooms.

Remember that training is a process, not an event, and it will take some time before your dog completely learns what you are trying to teach him, but he will surely make progress gradually with time.

Section Seven: Now What?

I need to tell you why I wrote this book. Dogology 101 was a great personal success. I was very, very proud of it, but I began to realize that people still had a ton of questions. They said they understood why I wrote Dogology 101. They understood the various reasons dogs do what they do, but they still did not comprehend how I could make dog training look so easy. Then, I began to realize it is because there is an art to it. No matter how cheesy that might sound, manipulating a leash and getting the dog proofed, getting the dog to respond to your voice is an art form. A form of art that comes naturally to you with time and an art that requires patience, structure, and a lot of determination.

Now some people will ask, if it comes naturally with time, then is there nothing they can do about it? What is the need of going through strenuous hours of mastering different skills of dog training and then days and days trying to teach those to your dog? But I believe that form of art will come if you keep working hard to train your dog with sheer willpower.

Another way that can make it easier for you to train your dog is to have good understanding between you and your dog, and that will only come when there is a strong bond between the two of you. And to create a bond of affiliation and love does take time, a lot of time, may it be the case of human to human bond or human to animal bond. The more time you two spend together, the better the bond between the two of you will be, making it easier for you to teach your dog and easier for the dog to understand and learn everything that you are teaching him. All you need to do is keep practicing the commands that you are trying to teach your dog without skipping a single day and be patient and always maintain one structure. As I mentioned, training is a process, not an event, and a process always takes time to complete and progresses gradually. So remember that patience and hard work are the two key aspects when you are trying to teach your dog any new command.

I have been practicing, and I have been patient with it for such a long time that it just comes to me naturally now whenever I am trying to teach anything to a dog. I wanted to document the process and then distribute it to other people to make living with a high energy dog easier and convenient and incident free. I also want people to understand that they are not alone. I struggle, even today, with Vodnik. I have struggled in the past with high energy dogs. There is nothing written out there that I have found that is useful, that actually breaks everything down, not just to a science, but to the art form of owning a high energy dog. It can be stressful from time to time and I get it, guys. But believe me that owning a dog that possesses high energy and is well trained about all the commands that are needed in our everyday life is beneficial and enjoyable.

Remember, as a dog trainer or even a dog owner, there are a lot of things that you must keep in mind before beginning to train your dog. You have to keep in mind that every dog does not have the same kind of quickness in learning. Some dogs learn fast while some others will take a little bit longer to learn any command that you are trying to teach him. Another thing to remember here is that you must not rush into any new thing that you are trying to teach to your dog because he will take some time to learn it. Patience is the key to success when you are training a dog. Without patience, if you rush things and give a lot of commands to your dog at the same time, he will probably be confused between which command to follow first and which comes next, and he will not be able to understand the difference between a positive command and a negative command when you rush things. In my point of view, if your dog does not know the difference between a negative command and a positive command, then all your training is just a total waste.

After you have completed training all the commands that you thought are a must for him, the process has not reached its end. You must not stop making him follow your commands or practicing those commands with him. As training makes a man perfect, so goes for a dog. The more he will practice the commands that you taught him, the easier it will get every day for you two. With practice, the reaction time of your dog will also increase, and he will be able to respond to your commands more quickly, which in my point of view, is one of the best things that you can accomplish from your training. The lesser the reaction time of your dog, the easier it will be for you to make him follow any command. Keep taking him on a walk daily like you did when you began the training because your dog has now gotten used to going out and following your commands, and he will need your directions to perform anything after the training. This is the main purpose of all the training that you have been giving him for a long time, and your training has proved to be useful after all.

Secret #20: New Variables

We have already gone over proofing, and along with that, we have gone over distractions while training our dogs any commands. There are other variables to training as well that we have not covered in distractions, such as the feeling of flooring for dogs. The dog will act differently on carpet than it does on linoleum or hardwood or even open grates. We have to get our dogs at least acclimated or introduced to these environments because we never know where we're going to be taking our dogs if we're good dog owners. But we need to practice for all variables. That means introducing it to new environments. If you're a non-smoker, go around people who vape or smoke. If you live in a one-story house, take your dog to family members or friends who live in a two-story or three- story home and have them at least experience looking down or looking up at stairs and then help them go up and down stairs. A wood porch might actually be difficult for dogs that only have a cement porch slab. Again, keeping in mind all the variables that we might encounter when bringing our dog out into the real world.

Variables Affecting Behavior

There are different variables present in our daily life that affect our dog's behavior towards the commands that we are giving him and the way he responds to them. . Some of them are listed below:

Surroundings & Distractions

The surroundings in which you trained your dog affect his behavior after you order him to follow a certain command. If you trained your dog in an environment where there were no distractions, it will be harder for him to follow your commands when you are working in a distracting environment. This is the main reason I always tell dog trainers to train their dogs about distractions because it will make them able to follow your commands anywhere regardless of the surrounding environment. Remember, when training your dog for distractions, always start from the least distracting environment and then move to the more distracting environment slowly.

Inherited & Acquired Traits

By acquired traits, I mean the traits that your dog learns throughout the training you were giving him. Inherited traits are the ones that come in the dog naturally through gene and breed. Different breeds of dogs have different inherited traits, but the same traits can be acquired through training. The better traits your dog has, the better his behavior towards your commands and in normal life will be. A dog with better inherited or acquired traits will be able to perform a task on a single command than another dog would perform after hearing the command two or three times.

Communication Variables

Your communication skills when training a dog matters a lot. When you are giving commands, you have to fashion your voice in such a way that your dog understands only from your tone the command you are giving is a positive command or a negative command.

Taking Vodnik for example here, I used to give him the positive commands in a slow and steady voice without any force. Similarly, when I wanted him to stop something, I would put some pressure on my voice, which made it louder and denser. Instantly, Vodnik knew that there is something wrong and he needs to stop doing that, which he eventually did. The better your communication, the easier it will be for your dog to follow your commands, and he will be able to understand them immediately, improving his behavior towards those commands and actions.

Diet & Health

Diet and health are two factors that contribute to one another to determine a dog's behavior. The better the diet of your dog, the better his health will be. The better his health, the more energetic he will be and more active towards the command that you are giving to him. It is really important to maintain a proper diet for your dog. Wrong diets can even lead to illness, which can be fatal sometimes. If you provide him a good diet and own a healthy dog, it will be amazing and fun training that dog and going out for walks or other places with him.

Reward Schedule

Treats are a must to give to your dog when training him because it makes him more interested and involved in the training, which makes the process easier and quicker. Remember that treats in a small amount more often are better than treats given in large quantity but less often. Less often makes the dog less attentive towards the present command that you are trying to teach him. It is better for one more reason to give the treats after short intervals. If you are giving your dog the treats in large quantity but less often, there is a chance that he might have done something wrong during the time interval difference from one treat to another, and he will still get a treat. It will make your dog unable to realize that he made a mistake and will probably do it again. He will be making the same mistake again and again because he did it the first time, and you fed him a reward by mistake or carelessly without noticing his mistake.

When you are giving treats after short intervals of time, you will be able to find his mistakes and restrict the treat at that moment. This will make your dog realize that there is something that he did not do right, so he did not get the treat and will try to find out and improve that mistake next time. This is one of the main benefits of giving your dog treats in small amounts more regularly than giving treats in larger amounts but less often.

Secret #21: Get Active

I hope you all agree that knowledge is something that always increases with sharing. The more you share it with others, the faster it would become for you as well. You see, it is a two way road; if you share your experiences and knowledge with others, they would reciprocate the same to you as well. Humans are social beings, and the more socially active they become, the better they get. This is also true in regard to your dog and problems you are facing with him or her. Maybe you could become the source of solving someone's problem. Being socially active never creates problems for you, and it surely would solve many of your problems as well as problems faced by others, who are in your circle, by virtue of your experiences.

I am a part of a lot of groups. I think being with people who are like minded, who want to improve daily not just themselves, but their families and their communities, helped me grow. This is where it gets even better, being social and finding people who share your interests and thinking and viewpoints to certain aspects of their lives. When you could find people who are just like you in this world, it is truly a blessing. This is the mindset that helped me find mentors who helped me improve and reach the point where I am today and then those people whose lives I affected for all the good reasons and positivity. These were the people I wanted to be around, the people who are like-minded to me and to whom I am the same. We can ask questions, get those questions answered, and do the same thing again and again, I feel like I belong to something bigger than myself when I am around these people. I am not by myself, but I am being much better than what I could have been otherwise, if I would have been sitting in my home, idling around.

It was by virtue of these groups and such people that gave me the encouragement to create an online page on Facebook, called Dogology University Alumni. The primary purpose that this page serves is that we are all people hailing from different parts of the world, and almost all of us are dog trainers, who have been training different breeds of dogs found all around the globe. Some people are new to dog training while others have been doing this for years now and have vast experience in the field, and when both these kinds of people meet, it becomes very easy for the newbies to learn things from the experienced trainers, instead of having their own bad experiences before learning things. They are always thankful to me for this awesome forum related to dogs and always happy because of the way everyone gets responses from others.

We get together, and we ask all sorts of questions. We are all in it together, just to make sure that we are giving our dogs the best that we could possibly give and they could possibly have. It could be questions about health; it could be questions about travelling with our dogs; it could be questions about diet and so on. It is obviously going to be about behaviors that we all face on a daily basis from our dogs. Again, you love your dog, but you have been told that it is too feisty to be a part of group classes. It is too aggressive to be around other dogs and at times risky, depending on the variety of behaviors shown by dogs. And just for the purpose of avoiding such problems, we have an online outlet for outreach and for support. We just want to give this invitation for you to go find us on Facebook and look for Dogology University Alumni.

For our current alum, we have our group walks for the dogs and their trainers where you can get together and get to know more about dog training and other dogs if you are in the local area. We are putting on group walks for charity purposes. We are doing group walks for health and refreshment and for socializing our dogs to be better equipped for day-to-day life activities, just being out in the real world.

Soon we will also announce the beginning of seminars where different dog trainers will be able to get together and then talk about their dogs and the common problems they face and try to find a solution to all those problems.

People may not understand how joining a social society is related to dog training. Well, there is actually a point behind joining it, and it is pretty evident. When you join other people who are on the same mission as you, you are able to learn more and learn quickly. You get to know different new things and new ways to improve your dog training. You get to know some of the common mistakes that you are making while training your dog to perform different commands. And when you are able to improve your mistakes, then the training becomes easier, and not only the training, but anything you try to improve gets better and easier. When fewer mistakes are made in the task that you are performing, the higher the chances of your dog learning more quickly, and surely, he will be able to learn more easily and eventually make the process easy for both of you.

When you join a social society related to the task that you are currently performing, you get to improve yourself every day. It helps you recognize your own weak points when you talk to other people, and it helps other people know the fields in which they have weak areas. You can then also probably find a solution to most of the problems that are commonly found among most dog trainers.

Secret #22: Further Education

Education and gaining knowledge, be it in any subject or walk of life, is a never-ending process. The deeper you go, the more aspects and horizons open to you. This has been the very basic secret that has helped humans to grow from the Stone Age to where we are now.

Understanding animals and their various behaviors is the same as well. I am always continuing my education. Eventually, I want to get my doctorate in communications. I'm all about self-improvement, further improvement, and higher education. I want my daughter to strive to go on to college and continue education beyond just an associate's or a four year degree. It's important for me to have something further for other people. If you feel like your dog needs more ... High energy dogs can't get by with just a couple walks a day or a group walk once a month. We have put together clubs for further education to strengthen the bond between you and your dog. Just doing things like scent work, or scent detection, where the dog is looking for fun odors, such as birch or clover, things that the AKC Scent Work trials provide, we have a club for that. You can also do further obedience, advanced obedience, like precision heeling for obedience trials. You can also join a rally club, which is the club for dogs to go through all the obstacle courses, and they don't have to be a purebred. Or, you can join the Dogology University Club, where we all meet up once a week, and we just have fun with our dogs. We go to a dog park. We toss some balls around, and we talk, we laugh, and we enjoy the company of each other's dogs.

Education is very important these days. You cannot compare someone who has a masters or PH.D. degree with someone who is uneducated. Education is must if you want to do anything in this world now. You will never find a uneducated person living a life full of luxuries and ease. Education also has a lot to do with the relationship between you and your dog. Education does not mean you need to get some kind of degree to train your dog. In fact, it means that you must have proper knowledge about different things, such as your dog's breed, habits, the training duration, patience, and other things related to the training of your dog.

Proper Knowledge of Commands

When you begin to train your dog, you must have proper knowledge of commands. There are two types of commands, negative commands and positive commands. Positive commands are the ones given to the dog to perform a particular task. Negative commands are the ones used to prevent or stop something, like the action that he is performing. It is very important for the trainer to have knowledge of these commands and know the difference between them. You should never mix up these commands. If you give a positive and a negative command to your dog at the same time, it will end up being confused as to which action to perform. That is why they should be given separately. Another thing to remember is that you should have separate words for negative and positive commands. If you are giving your dog a command to perform by using a word that you used to restrict him from a task, then he will probably end up thinking that you are ordering him not to perform that task.

Understanding & Utilization of "The 3 Ds"

The three D's of dog training are Distractions, Distance, and Duration. Distractions determine if your dog can follow your commands when he is being distracted by different types of distractions. It is important to train your dog to follow your commands, regardless of the distractions, because there are a lot of those present in the streets. Your dog must be able to follow your commands on the streets because that is the first identity of a well-trained dog. When your dog has mastered the training of distractions that means they've been proofed. They've been practicing, and you can be confident that, no matter what's going on, you can ask for a command and the dogs will perform this command.

The second D that you must have good knowledge about is distance. This is the distance between you and the dog. It's important if eventually we want to teach our dog off leash obedience. If you have given him the training of following your commands, no matter the distance between you and your dog, and had practiced it enough, then you can be carefree when you go out for a walk or have fun with your dog in the park and let him roam around without the leash on. Your dog will follow your commands on your one call, no matter the distance between you and your dog if he can hear your voice. You would not need to run behind your dog to reduce the distance between you and him and then give him the command to come to you because he does not listen to your commands from a far distance.

The third D that the trainer must understand is Duration. It is the time during which you train your dog new commands daily and the time during which you practice the old and the new commands. Remember that, when your dog is new to training, the duration must not be increased a lot at the very start. But you should begin from less duration and then keep increasing the duration slowly.

Conclusion

Always remember this: *"Newer problems and troubles mean progress!"*

This may seem lame to you without considering the context of it, but consider this, if you are facing a new problem or a new trouble has come to you, it obviously is a sign that you are moving ahead, new horizons and aspects are opening up to you, new revelations are revealing themselves to you. You are moving in the forward direction; that is why the old troubles, hindrances, and hitches are behind now, and a new chapter has started for you. And this type of thinking pattern and positivity is the very key that will take you to the doorstep of your success. All you need to do is be patient, be consistent, be determined, and be positive. If you will keep these by your side in the journey of learning and practicing, you will reach your destiny, if not today then tomorrow, or if not tomorrow, then day after tomorrow or someday very soon.

Dogs are the companions of humans in a way, at times, humans could not be. This is what makes them special, but if not trained properly and groomed to be well-mannered and disciplined, they can be the source of all your headaches by the ruckus they will create around you. In Dogology 202, I have tried my best to incorporate all the possible aspects that could help you train your high energy dogs in the most efficient manner possible and without going the long miles where they are not necessary, but you always need to bear in mind that this is not the case always, and at times, all your dog requires from you is to go another few miles to bring out the best of his behavior.

The first and most imperative of all would be your patience while training your dog. You know it is not only the training of your dog but your training as well. You need to be careful of your standing posture, your tone, your movements, and distraction levels in the environment during training sessions, and all these aspects are supposed to be catered by you. You need to learn about specific needs of your dog and how your dog differs from other dogs.

Patience is the key to the very first door. The very moment you lose it, you have compromised your progress. Losing your patience is just like throwing in the towel and accepting defeat and failure in the very start.

Then comes the consistency; the more consistent you are with your commands and training session, the more quickly results will follow and the more effective your training will be. Your consistency is what will consolidate your training sessions and help your dog remember your commands and what exactly is expected from a certain command. If you are not consistent, it would just mean that you are giving it all up in vain after achieving it.

Remember not to jump in directly and to go with a plan. Always go in after properly structuring your training sessions and carefully planning each and every thing. Be very thoughtful of each one of your actions and movements while training your dog, as a random action can lead to misunderstanding a certain command by your dog, and then everything will go down the sink hole, without you even realizing it at that point.

Never underestimate the usability and utility of training tools and aids and always use them after learning the right methodology to handle your dog with that tool. A leash is an important tool and should be considered an effective training aid. With its proper and effective use, one can avoid many hurdles and troubles, and it may lead to quicker and more effective results.

If you are good at something regarding dog training, always share your knowledge and useful tips with others and help them as much as possible and be as social as you can be. It will help you learn from other peoples' experiences and help others to learn from your experiences. Moreover, this would help people avoid going the long road and making the same mistakes as you had made and learn from your experience and avoid them. It is otherwise a proven proverb that sharing knowledge always increases it, instead of cutting it down, so be open about your failures and how you overcame them, so others may not have to go through those same mistakes.

This fact is imperative; while training your dog, you have to control your environment. You have to be very careful about the levels of distraction and anything that be acting as a distraction for your dog. Learning what may encourage your dog to obedience and quickly grasping new concepts and what may deter him from you or lead to reclusive behaviors is just as important as any other factor involved, and this art should be mastered by following the proper guidelines the best of which is to spend ample time with your dog and know him, know his likes and dislikes as you would know your child. This is what would help you conquer those fronts at which your dog differs from other dogs, or the regular secrets and tips to achieve a training target may not be successful in that particular regard; hence your observation and proper knowledge of behavioral traits of your dog will help you cater to those aspects.

Always be keen and careful of what you are saying and how you are speaking to your dog, avoiding a variety of tones for the same command etc., saving your dog from confusion and frustration. Always praise your dog for the right thing and take preventive measures for destructive and negative behavior.

Last, if you are constantly failing at a certain point and cannot inculcate a desired behavior in your dog even after several tries, keep yourself open to the option of seeking professional help and discussing your problem with someone with knowledge and experience.

I bid you guys good luck with your dogs.

And remember:

"Training Your Dog Shouldn't Feel Like Combat!"

Made in the USA
Monee, IL
03 January 2020